# How to Make a Movie

CRAFTED BY SKRIUWER

**Copyright © 2024 by Skriuwer.**

All rights reserved. No part of this book may be used or reproduced in any form whatsoever without written permission except in the case of brief quotations in critical articles or reviews.

At **Skriuwer**, we're more than just a team—we're a global community of people who love books. In Frisian, "Skriuwer" means "writer," and that's at the heart of what we do: creating and sharing books with readers worldwide. Wherever you are in the world, **Skriuwer** is here to inspire learning.

**Frisian** is one of the oldest languages in Europe, closely related to English and Dutch, and is spoken by about **500,000 people** in the province of **Friesland** (Fryslân), located in the northern Netherlands. It's the second official language of the Netherlands, but like many minority languages, Frisian faces the challenge of survival in a modern, globalized world.

We're using the money we earn to promote the Frisian language.For more information, contact : **kontakt@skriuwer.com** (www.skriuwer.com)

For more information, contact : **kontakt@skriuwer.com** (www.skriuwer.com)

# TABLE OF CONTENTS

## CHAPTER 1: UNDERSTANDING WHAT FILMMAKING IS ALL ABOUT

- What filmmaking covers: idea, script, shooting, editing, distribution
- Roles of producer, director, cinematographer, etc.
- Balancing creativity with planning
- Realizing different film types (shorts, features, documentaries)

## CHAPTER 2: PLANNING YOUR STORY & WRITING THE SCRIPT

- Finding and refining your core story idea
- Creating a script outline, synopsis, and logline
- Writing natural dialogue and shaping characters
- Formatting the script for clarity and industry norms

## CHAPTER 3: ORGANIZING THE BUDGET AND SCHEDULE

- Setting realistic budgets and contingency funds
- Breaking down the script for cost estimates
- Scheduling shoots effectively
- Balancing resources, time, and logistics

## CHAPTER 4: PUTTING TOGETHER A STRONG TEAM

- Defining key production roles (producer, sound mixer, etc.)
- Hiring or collaborating with reliable people
- Contracts, payment, and agreements
- Building a positive work culture

## CHAPTER 5: GATHERING THE RIGHT TOOLS

- Choosing cameras, lenses, microphones, and lights
- Renting vs. buying gear and managing backups
- Organizing equipment on set
- Ensuring safety and maintenance of tools

## CHAPTER 6: SIMPLE CINEMATOGRAPHY BASICS

- Framing shots and understanding camera angles
- Using the 180-degree rule and shot sizes
- Basic lighting setups and controlling exposure
- Maintaining continuity and a clean visual style

## CHAPTER 7: ADVANCED CAMERA TECHNIQUES

- Complex moves (dolly zoom, arc shots, whip pans)
- Focusing methods (rack focus, follow focus)
- Handling drones, gimbals, and multi-camera setups
- Integrating special rigs and advanced gear safely

## CHAPTER 8: LIGHTING BASICS AND METHODS

- Three-point lighting and natural vs. artificial light
- Balancing color temperature and mood
- Using reflectors, diffusers, and practical lights
- Planning night shoots and handling exterior scenes

## CHAPTER 9: CAPTURING SOUND ON SET

- The importance of clear dialogue
- Working with microphones (shotgun, lavalier, etc.)
- Eliminating noise and recording ambient sound
- Using booms, sound mixers, and managing gear

## CHAPTER 10: DESIGNING THE LOOK OF YOUR FILM

- Setting the visual tone through production design
- Dressing locations, using props, and maintaining continuity
- Costumes and wardrobe that match character and story
- Coordinating with the director and cinematographer

## CHAPTER 11: LEADING THE PRODUCTION AS A DIRECTOR

- Overseeing creative decisions and guiding the team
- Working with the AD for scheduling and daily operations
- Balancing time constraints with performance needs
- Solving on-set problems calmly and quickly

## CHAPTER 12: GUIDING THE ACTORS

- Helping actors understand character motivations
- Giving clear direction and constructive feedback
- Handling group scenes, emotional moments, and rehearsals
- Working with new or experienced talent

## CHAPTER 13: HANDLING A SMOOTH SHOOT

- Creating call sheets and daily plans
- Managing unexpected issues (weather, delays, gear failures)
- Keeping morale high with breaks and good communication
- Monitoring continuity, coverage, and daily progress

## CHAPTER 14: EDITING BASICS

- Organizing footage, syncing audio, and making assembly cuts
- Refining the rough cut, focusing on pacing and story flow
- Using transitions, cutaways, and basic audio edits
- Collaborating with the team and locking picture

## CHAPTER 15: ADVANCED EDITING TRICKS AND TECHNIQUES

- Match cuts, jump cuts, and parallel editing
- Using slow motion, speed ramps, and split screens
- Layered timelines, color adjustment, and compositing basics
- Polishing continuity, adding flair without distracting viewers

## CHAPTER 16: FINE-TUNING SOUND IN POST-PRODUCTION

- Cleaning dialogue, balancing music, and layering effects
- ADR, Foley, and ambience for richer audio
- EQ, compression, and panning to shape the soundscape
- Matching final mixes for different platforms

## CHAPTER 17: ENHANCING COLOR AND VISUAL EFFECTS

- Color correction vs. color grading
- LUTs, scopes, and matching scenes' looks
- Simple VFX (green screen, object removal, compositing)
- Keeping effects subtle and aligned with the story

## CHAPTER 18: PLANNING YOUR FILM'S RELEASE

- Setting goals and picking distribution paths
- Building early buzz with trailers and social media
- Navigating self-distribution, festivals, or streaming platforms
- Preparing press kits, handling local screenings, and marketing

## CHAPTER 19: FILM FESTIVALS AND NETWORKING

- Festival tiers, submissions, and premiere status
- Making the most of screenings, Q&As, and social events
- Building genuine connections rather than just handing out cards
- Using festival momentum to find distribution or future projects

## CHAPTER 20: STAYING IN FILMMAKING FOR THE LONG RUN

- Evaluating each project's lessons and staying updated
- Avoiding burnout and balancing career with personal life
- Exploring new genres, forming production companies, and growing a brand
- Developing a sustainable approach to filmmaking and continuous learning

# CHAPTER 1: UNDERSTANDING WHAT FILMMAKING IS ALL ABOUT

Filmmaking means making a film from start to finish. It includes steps like coming up with an idea, writing the script, gathering the right people and equipment, filming scenes, editing, and finally showing it to an audience. At first, it might seem like a big task. However, if you study the process, you can do it in a structured way. This chapter will walk you through what filmmaking involves, who is involved in the process, and what you need to keep in mind before you even write your first word of the script.

To begin, let's talk about what a film is. A film is a series of pictures shown quickly in order, creating the illusion of movement. When you add sound, dialogue, and music, you create a powerful tool for telling stories. People around the world watch films for entertainment, learning, or inspiration. Making a film can be done with different budgets. Some films cost millions of dollars. Others are made with almost no money, using a phone camera and free editing software. What matters is how well you plan and how much heart you put into the work.

## Why People Make Films

People make films for many reasons. Some want to tell a personal story that matters to them. Others enjoy the technical side of handling cameras and editing software. Some see filmmaking as a way to connect with others, share ideas, or possibly earn income. One of the most important things to remember is that your reason for making a film will guide your decisions. If your focus is on telling a small, emotional story, you might not need expensive equipment. If you want to create a huge action movie with special effects, you will need a bigger budget.

## The Major Steps of Filmmaking

Although every film is unique, most go through these major stages:

1. **Idea and Development**: You figure out what you want to say. You write it down in a short outline or summary.
2. **Pre-Production**: You turn your idea into a script. You create a plan for your budget and schedule. You also hire the main crew members and cast your actors.

3. **Production**: You film your scenes. You have your crew, equipment, and sets ready. You capture the footage needed to tell your story.
4. **Post-Production**: You edit the footage, work on the sound, add music, and do color correction or visual effects if needed.
5. **Distribution**: You share your film with audiences. This can be in movie theaters, on TV, or on streaming platforms. It can also be at film festivals or other events.

These stages are linked. The better you plan at the start, the easier filming and editing become. Every choice you make will affect how the final movie looks and sounds.

## Key People in Filmmaking

A successful film usually has a team of dedicated individuals. Small projects might see people wearing many hats, while big productions may have separate people for each job.

- **Producer**: Handles the budget, hiring, and scheduling. They are often involved from start to finish.
- **Director**: Manages the creative side. They decide how actors should perform and what shots to use.
- **Screenwriter**: Writes the script. Sometimes this is also the director or producer on smaller projects.
- **Cinematographer** (also called Director of Photography): Decides how to light and frame the shots.
- **Editor**: Takes all the footage and arranges it to form the final movie.
- **Production Designer**: Plans how the sets look. Works on locations, props, costumes, and more.
- **Sound Mixer**: Controls how sound is recorded on set and often works on improving it afterward.
- **Composer**: Writes music if the film has an original score.
- **Actors**: Perform the roles written in the script. They bring the characters to life.

Each person has a specific job, but they also need to work together to reach the same goal. Communication is key. If the cinematographer does not know the director's vision, the shots might not match the mood. If the sound crew doesn't coordinate with the camera crew, you might get bad audio.

## The Importance of Planning

Some new filmmakers want to pick up a camera and start shooting right away. While you can learn a lot by trying things on the spot, filmmaking is smoother with planning. If you create a solid script, know your budget, and schedule carefully, you can avoid many problems later. For instance, if you know you want to shoot a scene at sunset, you should note the time of sunset for your location and plan your shoot around it. If you forget, you might miss the light or be forced to change your plan.

## Balancing Creativity and Logic

Filmmaking is both creative and logical. On the creative side, you decide on story elements, visual style, and sound. On the logical side, you figure out how to stay on budget and meet your deadlines. Some might think creativity can't fit in a schedule, but that is not true. Having a plan lets you know how much time and money you have to explore new ideas. If you plan well, you can add extra touches that make your film special.

## Different Types of Films

Films come in many shapes and sizes:

- **Feature Films**: Usually 60 minutes or longer.
- **Short Films**: Under 40 minutes, often used by new filmmakers.
- **Documentaries**: Based on real events or people.
- **Experimental Films**: Focus on new ways of showing visuals and sound.
- **Commercial and Promotional Videos**: Designed for advertising or marketing.

Each type has different rules and expectations. A short film can give you practice before you tackle a bigger project. A documentary might need you to do lots of research. It's good to know what kind of film you want to make.

## Choosing an Idea

Every movie starts with an idea. Maybe you saw something interesting in your neighborhood. Maybe you thought of a fictional character in a strange situation. One good approach is to keep a small notebook or a phone app to record ideas as they come. After a while, pick the one that feels strongest or that you are most excited about. That will be the seed of your film.

## Building Confidence as a New Filmmaker

If you have never made a film before, you might feel nervous. That's normal. One way to build confidence is to watch many films and pay attention to how they are put together. Notice how scenes start and end. Notice how music affects your emotions. Study how the lighting changes from scene to scene. You can also read about filmmaking or watch behind-the-scenes videos. The more you learn, the more you'll feel at ease when you step on set.

## Working with a Low Budget

Lots of people think you must have tons of money to make a film. While money helps, creativity can make up for a smaller budget. For example, instead of renting a fancy studio, you might use a local spot that looks good for your story. You can also borrow gear from friends or local film groups. Many online sites allow you to download free sound effects or music. The main thing is to not spend more than you have.

## Making a High-End Film

Sometimes you have access to funds or contacts that let you make a bigger project. In that case, you can rent high-end cameras, hire experienced crew, and shoot on carefully built sets. But keep in mind, bigger budgets bring bigger responsibilities. You must keep track of more people, more equipment, and more details. The stakes are higher. If you mess up, you lose more money. Planning becomes even more important.

## Basic Legal and Safety Issues

Filmmaking also involves rules and regulations. You might need permission to shoot in certain places, like city sidewalks or public buildings. You might have to get a permit from local authorities. If you are filming a scene that involves stunts or special effects, you need to keep your cast and crew safe. Always follow safety rules. If your film has music, make sure you have the rights to use it. If you break these rules, you can face fines or lawsuits.

## The Role of Film in Society

Films are not just entertainment. They can shape how we see the world. They can introduce us to new ideas or different cultures. Some people make films to raise awareness about problems in society. Others try to make people laugh or cry. Understanding the power of film can help you make responsible choices. You can decide if you want your film to be purely for fun or if you want it to carry a deeper meaning.

## Technology in Filmmaking

Technology has changed how movies are made. Many people have a camera in their phone that can record high-resolution video. Editing software is more accessible now. You can store files on cloud platforms and share them with a team across the globe. Even if you are a student or just curious, you can experiment with these tools. Some of the biggest films still use advanced cameras, special effects, and large crews. But good stories can be told with simple tools if you know how to use them well.

## Common Mistakes to Avoid

- **Not planning shots**: Filming random clips without a shot list or storyboard can lead to confusion later.
- **Poor sound recording**: Audiences can handle low-quality video more than they can handle bad sound. Invest time in good audio.
- **Skipping backups**: Always save your footage in more than one place. Hard drives can fail.
- **Ignoring feedback**: Show your rough cuts to people you trust. Sometimes they spot problems you miss.
- **Overcomplicating**: Keep your story and shoot straightforward, especially if this is your first film.

## Keeping Control of Your Vision

When many people are involved, everyone has opinions. You might get advice on how to change your film. Some suggestions are useful. Others might go against your original plan. It's wise to keep an open mind, but also remember that you had a reason for picking this idea. Learn to listen to others while still preserving what makes your film unique.

## Real-World Example: Small Film, Big Impact

Sometimes, a small movie can become very famous. For example, certain independent films made on a tiny budget became hits at film festivals. They told strong stories that connected with viewers. These success stories remind us that you don't need a big studio behind you if you have a clear vision and determination to learn.

## Finding Your Style

A film's style is like its personality. It involves how you frame shots, the colors you use, the pacing of the scenes, and the way your actors perform. Some directors like slow, steady shots. Others prefer quick cuts and lots of camera movement. Some like bright, colorful scenes, while others prefer a more muted palette. Finding your style takes time. Watch other films, practice, and experiment.

## Handling Pressure

Filmmaking can be stressful. There are deadlines, budget constraints, and creative disputes. You might have only a few hours to shoot a scene before the light changes. Or you might have to reshoot if a key actor calls in sick. Learning to handle pressure involves staying calm, being flexible, and having a backup plan. Sometimes a problem can become a chance to try something new.

## What Makes a Film Good?

There is no single formula for what makes a film good. Different genres and styles appeal to different viewers. But there are some common points:

- **A good story**: Audiences like stories that make sense and have interesting conflicts.
- **Relatable characters**: Even in fantasy or science fiction, characters need human traits people can connect with.
- **Good pace**: Scenes should move along without dragging.
- **Clear sound and visuals**: If viewers can't see or hear what's happening, they lose interest.
- **Emotional impact**: Whether happy or sad, a film that makes people feel something is memorable.

## The Power of Collaboration

Collaboration is about working well with others. In filmmaking, you rely on many people to do their jobs correctly. You trust the cinematographer to capture great images, the sound team to record clean audio, the actors to give strong performances, and the editor to put it all together. If you want to be a good collaborator, communicate clearly, listen to feedback, and show respect for everyone's work.

## First Steps for a New Filmmaker

If you are starting out, here are a few simple actions you can take:

1. **Write down your film idea** in a single paragraph.
2. **Watch short films online** and analyze how they are made.
3. **Read about the basics of scriptwriting** (we will cover more in Chapter 2).
4. **Check what gear you have** (phone camera, basic editing software, etc.).
5. **Look for local film groups** or online communities to join.

These steps build a foundation. As you progress through this book, you will learn more about each part of filmmaking. Remember, everyone starts somewhere. Even the biggest directors once made their first short film.

## Seeing Filmmaking as a Learning Process

Every film you make teaches you something. You might discover you are good at editing, or that you prefer being behind the camera rather than in front of it. You might find you love writing scripts and you want to improve that skill. Treat every project as a step toward getting better. Take notes on what went well and what you could have done differently.

## Thinking About Who Will Watch Your Film

Before you start, ask yourself: who is this film for? Maybe it's a personal project only for friends and family. Maybe you want to put it on social media for your online followers. Or you might aim for film festivals. Knowing your audience can guide some choices, like how you structure the story or what format you release it in.

## Staying Organized

Good organization helps keep track of scripts, shot lists, schedules, and costs. Some people use spreadsheets or special software for film production. Even a simple folder system on your computer can help you find files quickly. Chaos can lead to missed deadlines or lost footage.

## Equipment Basics

In this book, we will talk about cameras, lenses, lights, tripods, microphones, and editing software. For now, remember that a good story and skilled people are more important than fancy gear. The best camera won't save a weak script, but the right story can shine even with modest gear if you use it well.

## Test Shoots

Doing a quick test shoot can help you see if your ideas work. You can film a short scene with actors or just shoot a location to see how the light looks. These test clips can also help you practice editing. This is a good way to find potential problems before you start the main shoot.

## Looking Ahead

As you read further, you will learn the details of scriptwriting, budgeting, scheduling, picking actors, and more. Each part is important. Skipping one area, like good sound recording, can cause big headaches later. A strong grasp of each step can make your film smoother and help you avoid simple mistakes. By the end of this book, you should feel ready to plan and shoot your own film.

---

### Chapter 1 Key Points Recap

- Filmmaking includes idea, pre-production, production, post-production, and distribution.
- It needs a team of people such as producers, directors, writers, editors, and more.
- You must balance creativity with planning and organization.
- Different types of films have different goals and requirements.
- It helps to know your audience and keep everything organized from the start.

This chapter gives you a broad understanding of filmmaking. Next, in Chapter 2, we focus on how to plan your story and write the script. That is the backbone of your film. Without a solid script, even the best camera or editing software won't help you craft a good movie.

# CHAPTER 2: PLANNING YOUR STORY AND WRITING THE SCRIPT

A good film starts with a clear story. A script is like a roadmap. It tells you what happens in each scene, what the characters say, and even where the action takes place. In this chapter, we will talk about how to plan a story, how to organize your thoughts, and how to write a script that makes sense to your team. We will cover basic script format, scene structure, and practical tips for writing dialogue. We will also touch on adapting a story from books or real events.

## Why a Strong Script Matters

No matter how impressive the visuals or sound are, a weak story can ruin a film. The script is important because:

- It helps the director plan shots and set the overall tone.
- It shows the actors what to say and how their characters change.
- It guides the entire crew on where the story is going so they can do their part.

If your script is confusing, everyone else will be confused too. So you want a clear script that captures your main idea and holds the audience's attention.

## Finding Inspiration for Your Story

You can find story ideas in many places:

- Personal experiences: Something you went through that might resonate with others.
- News stories: Events happening in the world that can form the basis of a drama or documentary.
- Books and comics: You might adapt an existing story if you have the rights to do so.
- History: Real historical events can form exciting plots.
- Daydreams: Let your imagination run. Sometimes a random thought can lead to a script.

The key is to look for something that makes you want to keep writing. If you lose interest halfway, your audience probably will too.

## Making a Logline

A logline is a one- or two-sentence summary of your film. It should include who the main character is, what they want, and what stands in their way. For example:

> *A young detective must solve a strange theft in a small town before the culprit sets off a bigger crime.*

This short statement clarifies the conflict and the stakes. You can use your logline to pitch your film to others or to stay focused as you write.

## Expanding into a Synopsis

After you have a logline, write a short paragraph or page describing the full story. This is called a synopsis. It helps you see the main events in order. You mention the beginning, middle, and end. You include major turning points. By writing a synopsis, you can see if the story flows or if you have a boring middle. This is a good time to fix problems before you write the full script.

## Building Characters

Characters are the heart of your film. People watch movies to see what happens to the characters. Here's how to build strong characters:

1. **Give them goals**: What does each character want? Maybe one wants money, another wants freedom, and another wants love.
2. **Give them obstacles**: Something or someone stands in their way.
3. **Give them traits**: Are they shy, brave, kind, or stubborn? These traits will affect how they react to events in the story.
4. **Show change**: Good characters learn or grow by the end of the film. Even in action movies, the hero often changes somehow.

Write down these details. Think about their backstory, but only show what matters. You don't have to tell the audience everything.

## Structure: Beginning, Middle, End

A common film structure is:

- **Act 1: Beginning** - Introduce the characters and the setting. Show the conflict or problem.
- **Act 2: Middle** - The main character tries to solve the problem, but faces bigger challenges.
- **Act 3: End** - The conflict reaches a peak, then resolves. The character learns a lesson or achieves a goal.

This three-act structure is not a hard rule, but it helps keep your story clear. It gives you a framework for planning the big events.

## Writing the First Draft

Your first draft is just getting the story out of your head and onto paper (or computer). Don't worry too much about small details or perfect dialogue. Focus on the main events and make sure the story is logical. Once you have a complete draft, you can go back and fix parts that don't work.

## Script Format Basics

Films generally use a standard script format. This helps actors, directors, and producers read it easily. Here are some basics:

- **Scene Heading (Slug Line)**: Tells you if the scene is inside (INT.) or outside (EXT.), where it is, and if it's day or night. Example:
  INT. LIVING ROOM – DAY
- **Action/Description**: A short paragraph explaining what happens. Write in the present tense. Example:
  The window rattles from a sudden gust of wind. The lamp flickers.
- **Character Name**: Written in uppercase when they speak. Example:
  MARIA
- **Dialogue**: What the character says. Example:
  MARIA (softly)
  I think the power is about to go out.

Keeping to this format makes the script easy to read. There are many scriptwriting software options that handle the formatting. Or you can do it by hand if you follow the guidelines.

## Scene Structure

Each scene should serve a purpose. It might show a key event, reveal character details, or heighten tension. Scenes that do nothing for the story can be cut. Ask yourself: does this scene move the plot forward or show something new about a character? If not, consider removing it.

## Dialogue Tips

- **Keep it simple**: People often speak in short sentences.
- **Show personality**: A character might have a unique way of talking. Maybe they use certain words often.
- **Avoid repetition**: Don't say the same thing multiple times.
- **Subtext**: Sometimes characters don't say exactly what they feel. A character might say "I'm fine" when they are actually angry.

## Descriptions

When you write descriptions in the script, focus on what the audience will see or hear. For example, don't write, "He remembers the time he fell off his bike when he was five." That memory won't be visible unless you plan to show it in a flashback. Instead, you might show him reacting nervously when he sees a bike. Let the audience figure out what that means.

## Adapting True Stories

If your film is based on real life, be aware that reality can be messy. You might need to change some details to make the story clearer or more interesting on screen. If you are telling someone else's story, you might need legal permission. Always check if you can use people's names and life events.

## Handling Multiple Drafts

Good scripts rarely come out perfect on the first try. You might write several drafts. In each draft, you fix the story flow, sharpen the dialogue, and remove parts that slow down the film. It's normal to have 5 or 10 versions of a script before you settle on the final one.

## Table Reads

A table read is when you gather some people (friends or actors) to read the script out loud. Hearing the dialogue spoken can show if it sounds natural. You might find places where the wording is clumsy or too long. You can also see how long the script might run.

## Getting Feedback

Ask for feedback from people you trust. They might spot plot holes or character issues you missed. Some might have suggestions to improve pacing or cut unnecessary parts. Remember, it's your script, so you don't have to follow every suggestion. But if many people point out the same problem, it might be worth fixing.

## Polishing Your Script

After gathering feedback, revise your script. Make sure it's free from major grammatical errors. Keep your scene headings consistent. Check that your dialogue sounds like actual speech. Ensure the story has a clear beginning, middle, and end. When you're done, you have a script ready for pre-production.

## Short Film Scripts

Short films usually run less than 40 minutes, so their scripts are shorter. You have to be concise. Focus on a single idea or event. Build up tension quickly, then resolve it. Short film scripts can be great for practicing. They also cost less to produce and can be entered into festivals.

## Feature Film Scripts

Feature scripts can run from about 80 to 120 pages (usually one page per minute). You have more time to develop characters and subplots. But you also need to keep the audience engaged for a longer time. Plan your major plot points carefully so there's no dull stretch.

## Genre Considerations

Different genres have different norms. A comedy script might have jokes in nearly every scene. A horror script might use more sound effects to build suspense. A science fiction script might need more descriptive scenes to show futuristic technology or worlds. Always keep the audience in mind. If you are mixing genres, do so in a clear way so viewers aren't confused.

## Common Script Problems

- **Overwriting**: Long paragraphs of description that slow down reading.
- **Too many characters**: Hard to follow who's who.
- **Weak conflict**: The main character's problems might not feel serious enough.
- **No resolution**: The film ends but leaves important questions unanswered (unless this is intentional).

## Example: How to Start a Scene

### Scene Heading:

EXT. LAKE – MORNING

### Action:

The sun glistens on the water's surface. A lone boat drifts near the shore. KYLE, early 30s, rows with uneven strokes, glancing over his shoulder from time to time.

### Dialogue:

KYLE (under his breath)
I hope they're not here yet.

This simple scene sets the mood: a quiet morning on a lake with a bit of suspense because Kyle is worried someone might arrive.

## Time Management During Writing

Some writers set a goal, like writing one page every day. Others prefer to write in longer blocks. Find a method that keeps you moving forward. If you wait until you feel "inspired," you might never finish. Discipline is key.

## Outlining Before Writing

Some writers outline every scene before writing. They list scene headings, what happens, and who's involved. This is called a step outline. It's like a skeleton of the movie. If you plan this way, you can spot issues in the story before you spend time writing full dialogue. On the other hand, some writers prefer a more free-flow approach. Pick the style that works best for you.

## Tools for Scriptwriting

- **Celtx**: Free or low-cost scriptwriting software.
- **Final Draft**: Industry-standard software for professional screenwriters.
- **WriterDuet**: Allows real-time collaboration online.
- **Highland**: A simple Mac-based writing tool.

You can also use regular word processors, but you'll have to manage formatting yourself. Some people use these tools not just for formatting, but also for story planning and scheduling.

## Protecting Your Idea

If you worry about people stealing your idea, you can register your script with official bodies (like the Writers Guild) if you live where that is possible. But keep in mind, many ideas are similar. Execution is what sets your film apart. If you have a strong script, it's harder for someone else to copy your unique approach.

## The Connection Between Script and Budget

When writing, keep in mind that everything you write has a cost. If you have a scene with a helicopter chase, that's expensive. If you have many special effects, your post-production budget will go up. If your budget is small, try to limit the number of locations or large action sequences. Write a script that you can afford to film. If you plan on a big budget, you can include bigger scenes, but be ready for the extra work and costs.

## Real-World Tip: Reusing Locations

If you only have access to one or two main locations, write the script around them. For example, if you have permission to use a local diner, set multiple scenes there. Change the look for different times of day to keep it interesting. This approach helps you save money.

## Putting the Script to the Test

Once you have a near-final script, share it with people who know your genre. If it's a comedy, see if they laugh. If it's a horror, see if they get tense. You can also share it with a small circle of trusted friends who can give honest input. This test run can reveal if your story is working.

## Knowing When the Script Is Ready

There's a saying: "A script is never finished, only abandoned." At some point, you have to stop making changes and move on. If you tweak it forever, you'll never shoot the movie. That doesn't mean you should rush. Polish it enough so it's strong. But be ready to let go once it's good enough to enter pre-production.

## Preparing for the Next Steps

After your script is done, you'll move to pre-production. This is where you hire crew, plan the budget, scout locations, and finalize the schedule. The work you did on your script will guide all these tasks. Knowing exactly what you need for each scene helps you plan effectively and avoid surprises.

## Chapter 2 Key Points Recap

- A strong script is crucial.
- Start with a logline, move to a synopsis, then to a full script.
- Use standard script format for clarity.
- Keep scenes relevant, and make sure each scene moves the story forward.
- Revise your script multiple times and get feedback.
- Plan your script according to your budget.
- Once the script is solid, you can move on to pre-production tasks.

With Chapter 2 complete, you now have a framework for your film's story. The next chapters will help you figure out how to organize your budget, schedule your shoot, hire the right people, and choose your gear. By the time you finish this book, you'll have a clear, step-by-step approach to making your movie come to life.

# CHAPTER 3: ORGANIZING THE BUDGET AND SCHEDULE

When you decide to make a film, you need to be realistic about how much money and time it will take. Budgeting and scheduling are major parts of pre-production. Even small mistakes in planning can cause big problems once you start shooting. This chapter will show you how to figure out how much money you need, where to get it, and how to use your time wisely. We will discuss basic terms, provide clear tips, and explain everything in simple language. By the end, you will know how to create a smart plan for your film's budget and schedule.

## 1. Why Budgeting Matters

Making a movie costs money. You have to pay for equipment, props, costumes, food for your crew, and many other things. Some films have tiny budgets, while others have budgets of millions of dollars. No matter how much you plan to spend, you need a clear budget.

- **Avoiding running out of money:** If you start filming without knowing your costs, you might run out of money halfway. Then you can't finish the movie.
- **Using money wisely:** A plan shows you where every dollar goes. This helps you decide which parts of the movie need more funding and which parts can manage with less.
- **Showing others you are organized:** If you want investors or sponsors, they will ask to see your budget. A tidy budget plan shows you have thought things through.

## 2. Basic Terms in Budgeting

Here are a few terms you might see:

- **Above-the-Line Costs:** These are costs related to key creative roles like the director, producers, and main actors. They often have set fees.
- **Below-the-Line Costs:** These cover everything else, like crew salaries, equipment, editing, sets, and so on.
- **Contingency:** This is money set aside for unexpected costs. A common contingency amount is 10% of your total budget.
- **Line Items:** Each separate cost in your budget is a line item (for example, camera rental, set construction, costume design).

---

## 3. Figuring Out Your Film's Needs

Before you can budget, you must know what your film requires. Make a list of the main elements:

1. **Script Requirements:** Does the story need a car chase? A special costume? A unique location like a beach or a desert? Each of these needs funds.
2. **Location Costs:** Some places charge fees to film. Others need permission or permits. Some might require security.
3. **Crew:** You will need camera operators, sound recordists, make-up artists, and so on. Each person might have a daily rate or an hourly rate.
4. **Equipment:** Cameras, lights, sound gear, and other tools may be rented or purchased. Rental is often cheaper if you only need them for a short time.
5. **Post-Production:** Editing, color correction, and sound mixing each have costs. If you need visual effects, that can add a lot to your budget.
6. **Food and Transport:** Cast and crew need meals. You might need a vehicle or bus to move everyone to different locations.

List each item, then try to guess how much it costs. You might have to do some research online or talk to friends who have made films before. If you are new, getting rough estimates is better than guessing randomly. Even if you can't be exact, having a list helps you avoid missing major costs.

---

## 4. Creating a Detailed Budget

Once you have a list, break your costs into categories:

- **Pre-Production Costs:** Fees for writers, location scouting, script changes, legal paperwork.
- **Production Costs:** Crew wages, equipment rentals, sets, props, costumes, location fees, transportation, food.
- **Post-Production Costs:** Editing, sound design, music licensing, visual effects, color correction.
- **Marketing and Distribution:** Posters, trailers, online ads, film festival submission fees, etc.

Under each category, write out specific line items. For instance, "Camera Rental" might be one line item. Next to it, put the estimated cost. This approach keeps things organized. You can use a spreadsheet or budgeting software. Some film production apps also help you manage these details.

---

## 5. Considering Different Budget Sizes

- **Micro-Budget (under a few thousand dollars):** You might rely on friends who work for free or minimal pay. You might film in locations you already have access to (like your home). You might use gear you or your friends own. These films often require more creativity to make up for the lack of funds.
- **Low-Budget (a few thousand to tens of thousands):** You can pay some of the crew, rent some gear, and maybe secure a few professional actors for short periods. You still have to be careful with spending.
- **Mid-Range Budget (hundreds of thousands):** You can hire a bigger crew, rent higher-end gear, and possibly use more complex sets or special effects. You have more room for reshoots if needed.
- **High Budget (millions):** Studios or large production companies often fund these. They hire top talent, build elaborate sets, and allocate large sums for marketing.

No matter your budget size, the process is the same: plan carefully and keep track of spending.

---

## 6. Golden Tips for Budgeting

1. **Use a Crew of Multi-Skilled People:** If a single crew member can handle both camera and lighting, you save money.
2. **Negotiate Equipment Rental:** Sometimes, you can negotiate a weekly or monthly rate that is cheaper than daily rates.
3. **Plan Shooting Days Efficiently:** More shooting days mean more expenses (crew wages, food, location fees). Keep your schedule tight but not impossible.
4. **Seek Sponsorship or Product Placement:** Some local businesses might give money or items if you feature their brand. Make sure this fits your film's style.
5. **Buy Used or Borrow:** For props, costumes, or small gear, check thrift stores or online marketplaces. This can cut costs dramatically.

---

## 7. Scheduling Basics

Along with your budget, you need a schedule that shows when each scene is filmed. A schedule helps you organize your cast, crew, and locations. It also helps you avoid wasting time. If your actor is only available for one weekend, you need to plan all of their scenes during that weekend.

---

**7.1 Script Breakdown**

A script breakdown is where you go through the script scene by scene and note every element required:

- Characters in the scene
- Props needed
- Wardrobe changes
- Locations and any special needs (for example, "night scene" or "rain effect")

Having a script breakdown helps you group scenes that use the same location or actors. This grouping saves time. Instead of going back to the same location multiple times, you schedule all those scenes together.

## 7.2 Shooting Schedule

Once you have the breakdown, create a shooting schedule. This schedule lists each day of production and which scenes will be shot. You might write something like:

- **Day 1:** Scene 1–3 at the park (morning), Scene 10 in the nearby café (afternoon)
- **Day 2:** Scene 4–6 at the house interior (morning), Scene 7 (afternoon)

Try to keep location changes to a minimum. Every move takes time. The schedule should also include breaks for meals. Also note if you need to shoot at a certain time for natural light (like sunrise or sunset).

---

## 7.3 Allowing for Extra Time

Things rarely go perfectly. An actor might arrive late. The weather might not cooperate. Equipment might break. Always leave some buffer time in your schedule. A common practice is to add at least one extra day for reshoots or unplanned delays, especially for longer projects.

---

## 7.4 Day vs. Night Shoots

Night shoots can be more expensive. You need extra lights, and crew members might charge more for working at odd hours. It also affects your cast's mood and energy levels. Plan night shoots only when they are truly important to the story.

---

# 8. Call Sheets and Daily Organization

A call sheet is a document sent out to the cast and crew before each shooting day. It tells them:

- Where and when to show up (call time)
- The scenes being filmed that day
- Special instructions (like wearing certain outfits or bringing specific items)
- Contact details for key people

Call sheets help everyone stay on the same page and avoid confusion.

## 9. Staffing and Time Blocks

When you hire crew members, you pay them for a certain number of hours or days. You want to use their time wisely. For instance, if your camera operator is only needed for half a day, do not bring them in for a full day unless you really need them around. That would waste money.

## 10. Keeping Track of Costs During Production

Even with a good budget plan, costs can change during filming. You might decide to buy a last-minute prop or rent an extra light. Keep a record of all extra expenses as they happen. Use a simple spreadsheet or dedicated software to note each payment. This lets you see if you are spending more than planned and adjust if needed.

## 11. Financing Your Film

Now that you know how to create a budget, you have to find ways to finance it. There are many options:

1. **Self-Finance:** You pay for everything yourself. This gives you full control, but it can be risky if the cost is high.
2. **Investors:** Individuals or companies might give you money in exchange for a percentage of profits. You need to show them a clear plan and a good script.
3. **Crowdfunding:** Websites like Kickstarter or Indiegogo let you collect small amounts from many people. Offer perks like special thanks or signed posters to attract backers.
4. **Grants:** Some arts or film organizations give grants if your project meets their criteria. You often have to apply with a proposal.
5. **Partnerships:** Sometimes local businesses or even government bodies might sponsor you if your film promotes their city or aligns with their goals.

## 12. Dealing with Unions

Depending on where you live, your actors or crew might belong to unions. Unions have rules about wages, working hours, and breaks. If you hire union members, factor union rules into your budget and schedule. If you can't meet those requirements, consider working with non-union talent, though that might limit your options if you want big-name actors.

## 13. Location Permits

If you plan to film in public spaces, you might need permits from local authorities. Permits can cost money, and getting them can take time. This is another reason to start your planning early. If you skip permits, you risk being shut down by the police, which could derail your schedule.

## 14. Insurance

Film insurance can cover accidents or damage to equipment. If someone gets hurt on set, insurance helps pay medical costs. Some locations require you to have insurance before they let you film. The cost of insurance depends on the level of risk. If your film has stunts or special effects, the cost might be higher. Always factor insurance into your budget if your production is more than a small home project.

## 15. Planning for Post-Production

Many people think about production costs but forget post-production. Editing, color correction, sound design, and music all need money. If you plan to hire a professional editor or rent a recording studio, put those costs into the budget. Also, book the editor or post-production team early, so they can reserve time for your project.

## 16. Scheduling Post-Production Time

Once filming ends, you need to edit all your footage. This can take weeks or months, depending on the length of your film and how complex the edits are. Create a post-production schedule. Decide what needs to happen first. Usually, you start with a rough cut, then move to sound, then color correction. If you have visual effects, you might run them in parallel. Communicate with your editor or team to make sure everyone knows the deadlines.

---

## 17. Avoiding Burnout

Long production days can be tough on everyone. Schedule rest days, especially if your film shoots last more than a week or two. Tired people make mistakes, and that can slow things down or increase costs. If you treat your cast and crew well, they will work better and help you get good footage.

---

## 18. Revising the Schedule

Schedules often change. A location might not be available on the planned date. An actor might have a conflict. If changes happen, update your schedule right away and inform everyone. Use emails, messaging apps, or calls to make sure no one is left out. Keep track of each version of your schedule so you know what changed.

---

## 19. Communication with Your Team

During pre-production, hold regular meetings or calls with your producer (if that's not you), director, and department heads (like cinematography or wardrobe). Go through the budget and schedule so everyone knows the plan. Encourage them to speak up if they see any potential problems or ways to save money. Early communication can prevent big issues later.

## 20. Planning for Contingencies

Set aside a little extra money for unexpected events. Maybe you need more time for a scene that is crucial to the story. Without contingency funds, you would have to remove or shorten that scene. Also, have a backup plan for locations or props. If a location becomes unavailable, know where else you can film.

---

## 21. Distribution and Marketing Budgets

Though this will be covered in more detail in later chapters, it is smart to set aside a portion of your budget for distribution and marketing. Even if you plan to release your film online for free, you might need some funds for promotional materials or festival fees. If you hope to show your film in theaters, marketing becomes even more important.

---

## 22. Tools and Software

There are a few software tools that can help with budgeting and scheduling:

- **Movie Magic Budgeting:** A popular tool in professional film circles, but can be expensive.
- **Celtx:** Offers budgeting and scheduling features in addition to scriptwriting tools.
- **Google Sheets or Excel:** Simple spreadsheets work fine if you're on a small budget.
- **Trello or Asana (for scheduling tasks):** Good for tracking tasks and deadlines.

Pick the tool that fits your project size and your comfort level. Remember, the best tool is the one you actually use.

---

## 23. Step-by-Step Summary

Here's a short list of what you need to do for budget and schedule:

1. **Break down your script** to see all your needs.

2. **List your line items** (crew, props, gear, etc.).
3. **Estimate costs** for each item. If unsure, do research or ask for advice.
4. **Add a contingency** fund (5–10%).
5. **Arrange a shooting schedule** that groups similar scenes and respects everyone's availability.
6. **Create daily call sheets** during filming to keep everyone on track.
7. **Monitor spending** daily to ensure you're within your budget.
8. **Update the schedule** if anything changes.
9. **Keep everyone informed** at all times.

---

## 24. Real-World Example: A Short Film with Limited Money

Let's say you have a short script that takes place mostly in a single living room. You have a small crew of four: a camera operator, a sound person, a lighting assistant, and a director who also wrote the script. You plan to shoot over two days. Here's how you might break things down:

- **Location:** Use your own living room for free.
- **Camera Gear:** Borrow a camera from a friend. Rent lights from a local shop for two days at a discounted rate.
- **Food:** Budget for lunches and snacks for four people.
- **Actors:** Two local actors who agree to work for a small fee and credit.
- **Transport:** Everyone drives themselves, and you reimburse gas for the two actors.
- **Post-Production:** The director will do basic editing on free software. Sound person will help with cleaning up audio.

Your schedule might look like this:

- **Day 1 (morning):** Scene 1–2, set up lights, do tests.
- **Day 1 (afternoon):** Scene 3–4.
- **Day 2 (morning):** Scene 5–6.
- **Day 2 (afternoon):** Scene 7, plus any pickups or reshoots.

You set aside a small extra fund in case a light breaks or if you need to rent something else last minute. This is a basic example, but it shows how planning ahead makes everything run smoothly.

## 25. Staying Flexible

No matter how well you plan, things can change. A budget or schedule is a guide, not a rigid rule. If you see that a certain cost is too high, you might rewrite the scene to reduce that cost. If you finish filming a day early, you can use that time to shoot an extra scene or work on test shots. Being flexible helps you adapt without losing control of the project.

---

## Chapter 3 Key Points Recap

- Budgeting and scheduling are about controlling money and time.
- Make a clear list of every item you need.
- Think about above-the-line and below-the-line costs.
- Use a script breakdown to create an efficient shooting schedule.
- Keep extra funds (contingency) for surprises.
- Communicate changes to everyone involved.
- Use tools (spreadsheets or dedicated software) to stay organized.

When you finish this process, you have a realistic idea of how much money you'll need and how many days it will take to shoot your film. You have laid the foundation for a smooth production. Next, in Chapter 4, we will talk about building a strong team. Good people are the engine of any film project, so finding the right crew and understanding how to work with them is crucial.

# CHAPTER 4: PUTTING TOGETHER A STRONG TEAM

A film is not made by one person alone. You need a set of dedicated individuals who each do their part to bring the story to life. In earlier chapters, we looked at the roles of producer, director, writer, cinematographer, and more. Now, we will discuss how to find good people to fill these roles and how to manage them so that the production runs smoothly. A strong team can solve problems, add valuable ideas, and make the entire process more fun. This chapter will also share some little-known bits of advice for working with people at different skill levels.

## 1. Why Teamwork Is Important

When many people work together, there needs to be coordination. If one department fails, the whole film suffers. For instance, if the sound team misses important audio, it won't matter how good the visuals are. If the cinematographer doesn't show up on time, you lose precious hours of shooting. Good teamwork means each person understands their job, respects deadlines, and communicates well with others.

## 2. Defining Key Roles

Let's take a closer look at some key roles:

1. **Producer:** In charge of the overall project, often handles money and scheduling. Sometimes the producer is the person who initiated the project.
2. **Director:** Guides the creative vision, works with actors, and decides how scenes should look and feel.
3. **Cinematographer (Director of Photography):** Plans the camera work and lighting to achieve the desired visual style.
4. **Production Manager:** Oversees day-to-day operations, including budgets, location arrangements, and schedules.

5. **Sound Mixer or Sound Recordist:** Handles microphones, sound levels, and ensures clean recordings.
6. **Production Designer:** Creates the look of the sets, locations, and props.
7. **Make-up Artist and Costume Designer:** Responsible for how actors appear on camera, from outfits to hair and make-up.
8. **Editor:** Works in post-production, assembling footage to form the final movie.
9. **Boom Operator:** Holds the boom microphone for recording dialogue on set.
10. **Gaffer:** In charge of the electrical department and practical lighting.
11. **Grip:** Helps with lighting setup, rigging, and moving camera equipment.

Smaller productions might combine some roles. For example, the cinematographer might also be the camera operator. The director might also be the writer. But for larger projects, each role can be filled by a separate person.

---

## 3. Hiring or Recruiting

**Where do you find these people?**

- **Film Schools:** Students or recent graduates often look for hands-on experience.
- **Online Communities:** Sites or social media groups dedicated to filmmaking can help you connect with interested people.
- **Local Events or Meetups:** Some towns have film clubs or monthly gatherings where filmmakers talk about projects.
- **Referrals from Friends:** Word of mouth is a common way to find dependable crew.

When you find candidates, ask about their past experience. If you are hiring for a key role like cinematographer, watch samples of their work. If you have a small budget, you might find someone who is willing to work for a lower rate or for credit. Just be clear about expectations from the start.

## 4. Interview and Selection Process

When building your team, do a simple interview. It can be a phone call, video chat, or casual meeting:

1. **Ask about goals:** Why do they want to work on this film?
2. **Discuss availability:** Can they commit to the schedule you have?
3. **Check reliability:** Do they have references or past projects you can look at?
4. **Share your vision:** Explain the tone and style of the film. See if they are excited about it.

It's important not just to hire someone with the best technical skills, but also someone who works well with others. A brilliant but rude individual can harm team spirit.

---

## 5. Paying Your Team

Payment depends on your budget. Some small films rely on volunteers or low pay. Others pay union rates. Always be honest about what you can offer. If you can't pay much, consider providing meals, transportation, or even small perks like a copy of the finished film for their portfolio. For bigger productions, you need contracts that outline wages, payment schedules, and work terms.

---

## 6. Contracts and Agreements

Even if you are working with friends, it's wise to have written agreements. This can be an email or a simple document stating:

- The role and responsibilities of the person.
- The start and end dates of their work.
- The payment or benefits they will get.
- Any other important details, like ownership of footage or confidentiality.

Written agreements prevent misunderstandings. If any dispute arises, you have a document to refer to.

## 7. Building a Positive Work Culture

You want your cast and crew to stay motivated. A positive atmosphere helps everyone do their best. Here are some tips:

- **Treat everyone with respect:** Greet people by name, listen to their ideas, and thank them for their work.
- **Provide decent meals:** Hungry crew members can't focus well. Offering healthy snacks and meals is a small cost compared to the benefit of keeping morale high.
- **Keep the set safe and organized:** Clearly mark cables, set up signs for restricted areas, and follow safety procedures. If people feel safe, they can focus on doing good work.
- **Encourage open communication:** If a crew member notices a problem, they should feel comfortable telling you. That feedback can prevent bigger problems later.

---

## 8. Setting Clear Expectations

From the start, explain to each crew member what your project is about, how long it will take, and what their tasks are. If your schedule is tight, let them know. If they are expected to stay late, tell them in advance. Surprises can lead to frustration. A short meeting or a written summary can clarify everyone's job.

---

## 9. Special Roles You Might Overlook

Some roles seem small but can make a big difference:

- **Script Supervisor:** Tracks continuity, making sure details (like props, clothing, or actor movements) match between shots.
- **Production Assistant (PA):** Helps with small tasks on set, like running errands, getting coffee, or carrying gear.
- **Location Manager:** Finds suitable filming spots and handles permits or local agreements.

Having these support roles covered keeps the production running smoothly. Even small tasks, if left undone, can slow everyone else down.

## 10. Working with Actors

Actors need a special kind of attention. Here are some ways to support them:

- **Give them a clear script:** They should know their lines and scene objectives.
- **Provide a comfortable waiting area:** Actors often wait between shots. A quiet place can help them stay focused.
- **Respect personal boundaries:** Some scenes may require emotional vulnerability. Communicate clearly and always respect the actor's comfort level.
- **Offer simple direction:** Speak plainly about what you want. If they are confused, take time to discuss the character's motivation or the situation in the scene.

A good director-actor relationship is built on trust. If the actor trusts the director, they feel free to try new things and deliver better performances.

## 11. Managing Different Personalities

On set, you might have people with big egos or very shy natures. A film set can be stressful, and stress can make personalities clash. Here are suggestions:

- **Stay calm:** If someone is upset, raising your voice back won't help. Talk to them privately, understand their concern, and see if there's a solution.
- **Offer praise when deserved:** People like to feel valued. Notice good work and mention it.
- **Address issues early:** If two crew members don't get along, handle it sooner rather than later. A calm chat with both might fix the problem before it gets worse.

If the conflict is severe, you might have to replace a team member. But always try to find a fair and peaceful resolution first.

## 12. Training and Workshops

For a complex shoot, you might need people who understand certain equipment or techniques. If your budget allows, consider hosting a short training session. For example:

- A camera workshop for production assistants who might help the cinematographer.
- A safety briefing for stunts or special effects.
- A short class on how to operate a sound recorder properly if you have a small crew.

This training ensures everyone knows the basics, which can boost efficiency on set.

---

## 13. Delegation Skills

A director can't do everything alone. Learn to delegate tasks to the right people. If you have a production manager, trust them to handle some scheduling details. If you have a cinematographer, let them pick the lenses and lights. Micromanaging can slow things down. Instead, give clear goals and trust your team's expertise.

---

## 14. Team Communication Tools

In modern filmmaking, you can use apps and platforms to keep everyone informed:

- **Group Chats (WhatsApp, Slack, etc.):** Quick way to send announcements, share location details, or post schedules.
- **Shared Calendars:** Everyone can see the shooting schedule in real time.
- **Email Updates:** Useful for sending call sheets, scripts, or large files.
- **Video Conferencing:** If team members are in different places, schedule virtual meetings for updates.

Pick tools that your team is comfortable using, and keep your communication clear and timely.

## 15. Respecting Crew Expertise

Each crew member is a specialist. The sound recordist knows how to get the best audio. The make-up artist knows how to style hair for the camera. Sometimes a director might have a specific idea, but it conflicts with a crew member's expertise. Talk it through:

- Explain your vision for the scene.
- Ask the crew member for their input.
- Find a solution that respects both the creative goal and technical needs.

This cooperation creates a strong bond and usually a better result on screen.

## 16. Handling Emergencies on Set

Things can go wrong: an actor might get sick, or an important piece of equipment might break. Have a plan:

- **Emergency Contacts:** Keep phone numbers for local clinics or hospitals.
- **Backup Equipment:** If you can afford it, have a backup camera or at least spare batteries and memory cards.
- **Stunt or Safety Plan:** If you have stunts, have a trained safety person on set.

If an emergency happens, stay calm and follow the plan. It's better to lose a few hours of shooting than to put someone at risk or continue with broken gear.

## 17. Working with Volunteers

Some projects rely on volunteers who want to learn or be part of the experience. While this can save money, volunteers might have limited time or skill. Treat them kindly and show them how to do basic tasks. Make sure they understand what they signed up for. If possible, pair volunteers with experienced crew members so they can learn on the job.

## 18. Cultural Sensitivity and Respect

Film sets can bring together people from different cultures or backgrounds. Be mindful of words or behavior that might offend someone. Encourage an inclusive environment where everyone feels comfortable. This respect can prevent misunderstandings and create a healthier work atmosphere.

---

## 19. Managing Remote Collaborators

Sometimes you can't have everyone on set or in the same city. You might have a composer who lives far away or an editor who works from home. Communicate clearly with them using video calls or emails. Share your visual and audio files through online storage. Set clear deadlines for when you need the music or edited footage. Remote collaboration can be smooth if you plan it well.

---

## 20. Rewarding Team Members

Even if you can't pay large amounts, you can still show appreciation. You could:

- Provide a wrap party with some snacks and music to say thanks.
- Write personalized thank-you notes to each crew member.
- Mention them in social media posts, highlighting their work.
- Give small gifts that relate to the film (like a prop or a signed poster).

People like to feel valued. Showing gratitude boosts their memory of the project and might encourage them to work with you again.

---

## 21. Leading by Example

If you're the director or producer, people look to you for leadership. Show up on time, treat everyone politely, and be prepared. Your actions set the tone for the rest of the team. If you lose your temper or act disorganized, others might do the same. Keep calm, stay positive, and focus on solutions.

---

## 22. The Role of Rehearsals

If you have time, set up rehearsals for complex scenes or for big group scenes. This lets the actors get used to their lines and blocking. The cinematographer can plan camera moves, and the sound team can test microphone placement. Rehearsals reduce surprises on the actual shoot day. They also help everyone become familiar with each other's working styles.

---

## 23. Resolving Disputes

Disagreements are normal when creative people work together. A cinematographer might want a moody lighting setup, while the director wants a bright scene. An actor might suggest a different approach to the dialogue. Handle disputes by:

1. Listening to each side's reasoning.
2. Checking if the change still fits the film's story.
3. Making a decision that keeps the film's main idea in mind.

Sometimes you compromise. Other times, you stick to the director's final call. The key is to handle it professionally, without anger or insults.

---

## 24. Keeping the Environment Friendly

In stressful moments, remember you are all trying to make something creative. Encourage breaks where people can chat or relax for a few minutes. Small gestures like having a coffee machine or a snack table can lift spirits. A team that is treated well generally produces better results.

---

## 25. Reviewing Team Performance After the Project

When the production wraps, take time to review how things went:

- What worked well with your team?
- What could be improved?
- Who excelled in their role and might be great to re-hire later?

You might do short exit interviews or gather feedback by email. This information helps you build an even stronger team for your next film. It also helps you maintain a good network of people for future projects.

---

## Chapter 4 Key Points Recap

- Hiring the right crew involves knowing each role and finding people who fit the project's needs.
- Clear agreements and good communication prevent misunderstandings.
- A positive work culture boosts morale and reduces conflicts.
- Respect each person's expertise, but also keep the film's main idea in focus.
- Plan for emergencies, treat volunteers well, and show appreciation to the entire team.
- Keep track of performance so you know who to work with again.

With a strong team in place, you are much more likely to complete your film on schedule, within budget, and with fewer headaches. In the next chapters, we will look at gathering the right tools and learning the basics of cinematography. The technical side of filmmaking can be just as important as the creative side, and you will see how teamwork and good planning help you get the best results from your equipment.

# CHAPTER 5: GATHERING THE RIGHT TOOLS

You have your script, you have a team, and you have a plan for the budget and schedule. Now you need the equipment that will help you bring your film to life. This chapter covers essential tools for shooting a film, including cameras, lenses, sound gear, lighting, and other helpful items. You will see that having the newest or most expensive gear is not always the key. The real key is choosing tools that match your project's needs. We will also look at how to rent or borrow gear, how to keep it organized, and how to prepare backups. By the end, you should have a clear idea of what you must get before production starts.

## 1. Camera Choices

Cameras are often the first thing people think about when they hear "filmmaking tools." There are several types of cameras, each with pros and cons. It's not about the "best" camera; it's about the right camera for your story and budget.

1. **DSLR or Mirrorless Cameras**
    - These are commonly used by small crews or independent filmmakers. They can record high-quality video, often in 4K.
    - They have interchangeable lenses, so you can switch between wide, normal, and telephoto lenses.
    - They are relatively light, making them good for handheld work or small stabilizers.
    - Battery life can be limited, and they sometimes have record time limits.
2. **Cinema Cameras**
    - These are designed mainly for movie production. They often have higher bit rates, better color depth, and more control over settings.
    - They might record in formats that allow for easier color correction in post-production.
    - They can be more expensive, and the files they produce can be large.

- You'll likely need extra gear like an external monitor or a rig.
3. **Camcorders**
    - These were popular for home video but can be used for documentaries or simple shoots.
    - They might have smaller sensors, so the image quality might be less cinematic.
    - They can be more convenient if you just want a quick setup without swapping lenses.
4. **Smartphones**
    - Modern phones can shoot high-resolution video. Some indie films have been shot entirely on phones.
    - The main advantage is portability and ease of use.
    - The downside is that you have limited lens options, and the sensors are small, so low-light performance might not be great.

No matter which camera you pick, make sure you know how it works. Study the settings, practice filming test clips, and see how the footage looks on your computer or monitor. Experiment with frame rates (24fps, 30fps, 60fps, etc.) and resolutions (1080p vs. 4K) to find what suits your film. Also, plan to have enough memory cards and batteries on set.

---

## 2. Lens Basics

Lenses affect how your image looks more than many people realize. Even if you have a good camera, the lens can make a big difference. Lenses affect the field of view, depth of field, and sharpness.

1. **Focal Length**
    - Wide-angle lenses (like 18mm or 24mm) capture more of the scene. They can also cause some distortion around the edges if you get too close to your subject.
    - Normal lenses (around 35mm or 50mm on many cameras) give a view somewhat close to how human eyes see.
    - Telephoto lenses (like 85mm, 100mm, 200mm, etc.) zoom in on distant subjects and can create a nice blurry background (shallow depth of field).
2. **Prime vs. Zoom Lenses**

- **Prime lenses** have a fixed focal length (for example, 50mm only). They are often sharper and have wider apertures (allowing more light).
- **Zoom lenses** can change focal length (for example, 24-70mm). They offer more flexibility, especially if you don't have time to swap lenses between shots.

3. **Aperture (f-stop)**
    - The aperture controls how much light the lens lets in. A lower f-stop number (like f/1.8) means a larger opening and more light. This also gives you a shallower depth of field (blurrier background).
    - In low-light situations, a lens with a low f-stop is very helpful.

When choosing lenses, think about the type of scenes in your script. If you have a lot of wide shots of landscapes, you might want a good wide-angle lens. If you have many close-up shots of people's faces, maybe a medium telephoto lens is ideal. Don't forget the budget. Quality lenses can cost more than cameras, but you can often rent them if needed.

---

## 3. Audio Gear

Great visuals are nice, but bad audio can ruin a film. Microphones capture dialogue and ambient sounds. You need to plan carefully for audio gear.

1. **Shotgun Microphone**
    - These are long, narrow microphones that pick up sound mainly from the front and minimize noise from the sides. They're often mounted on a boom pole.
    - They help capture clear dialogue if aimed correctly.
    - They can be attached to the camera, but it's better to keep them close to the actor's mouth, just outside the frame.
2. **Lavalier (Lapel) Microphones**
    - Small mics you can clip to a person's clothing.
    - Good for interviews or when you want hidden mics.
    - Some are wireless, allowing actors to move freely.
3. **Handheld Recorder**
    - Sometimes you might want a separate audio recorder that can record high-quality audio.

- This is common in documentaries or when you can't have a big setup.
4. **Audio Interface or Mixer**
    - If you have multiple microphones, a mixer helps control levels.
    - A dedicated audio interface can record sound onto a separate device rather than into the camera.

If you record audio separately from the camera, remember to slate or clap at the start of takes so you can sync the audio in post-production. Check your levels to avoid distortion. Always have extra batteries for your audio gear.

---

## 4. Lighting Equipment

Lighting is crucial for shaping the mood and making sure your actors are clearly visible. Different types of lights serve different purposes.

1. **LED Panels**
    - LED lights are cool to the touch, energy-efficient, and often dimmable.
    - They can come in different color temperatures, like daylight or tungsten. Some let you adjust color temperature.
    - They're portable and good for small to medium shoots.
2. **Tungsten Lights**
    - These have a warmer color (around 3200K).
    - They can get very hot, and they use more power.
    - They're good for a classic film look or for matching interior lighting.
3. **Fluorescent Lights**
    - They give a soft light and don't heat up much.
    - They can flicker if not matched with the correct shutter speed, depending on your camera settings.
4. **HMI Lights**
    - Very bright, often used for daylight scenes or large sets.
    - They can be expensive to rent or buy.

You don't always need a huge lighting kit. With the right placement and some light modifiers (diffusers, reflectors, flags), you can achieve a professional look even on a budget. Sometimes, you can use natural light from windows, but you must plan for the sun's position. If you rely on sunlight, keep an eye on the weather and time of day.

## 5. Grip Gear and Accessories

To keep your shots steady and well-framed, you need some grip gear. Here are a few common items:

- **Tripods:** A stable tripod keeps the camera from shaking. Get one that can handle your camera's weight.
- **Shoulder Rigs:** Let you move around with the camera on your shoulder while reducing wobble.
- **Sliders:** Let you move the camera smoothly on a short track, for small, controlled moves.
- **Dollies:** For more complex tracking shots. Some dollies need tracks on the floor, while others have wheels that roll on smooth surfaces.
- **Stabilizers/Gimbals:** Electronic devices that keep the camera stable even as you walk or run.

For lighting, you might need C-stands (sturdy stands that hold lights or flags) and clamps to attach reflectors or diffusion material. These might seem small details, but they are important for controlling your shot quality.

---

## 6. On-Set Essentials

Beyond the main gear, there are various smaller items that can make your life easier:

- **Gaffer Tape:** A strong tape that doesn't leave residue. Useful for labeling, marking the floor, or taping down cables.
- **Sandbags:** Keep your light stands or tripods from tipping over.
- **Extension Cords and Power Strips:** You might need multiple power outlets.
- **Memory Cards and Hard Drives:** Store your footage safely. Always have backups.
- **Batteries and Chargers:** You will likely burn through more batteries than you expect.
- **Headphones:** So your sound person can monitor audio properly.
- **Cleaning Kits:** To keep lenses and sensors free of dust.

Having these items ready saves time. You don't want to stop filming just because a cable is too short or a stand tips over due to wind.

## 7. Renting vs. Buying

Deciding whether to rent or buy gear depends on your budget and how often you plan to use the equipment:

- **Buying**
    - You have the gear for as long as you want.
    - Good if you plan multiple projects.
    - Larger initial cost. You must maintain it.
- **Renting**
    - You can get high-end gear you might not afford to buy.
    - Great for short-term use or one-off shoots.
    - You must return it on time. Late returns can be expensive.
    - Rental fees add up if you keep the gear for too long.

Some people choose a mix of both. They might buy a basic camera and lens but rent a special lens or a large light kit for big scenes.

---

## 8. Borrowing or Sharing Gear

If you have friends or connections in film, you might borrow gear. This can reduce costs. Be responsible with borrowed equipment. Handle it with care, and return it on time. Offer to pay for any damage or wear you cause. Alternatively, you can share gear in a small group of filmmakers, splitting costs. This arrangement can work well if everyone communicates clearly about when they need the equipment.

---

## 9. Testing Your Equipment

Never wait until the first day of shooting to turn on your gear for the first time. Test everything in advance:

- **Check camera settings:** Make sure you know how to adjust ISO, aperture, frame rate, and white balance.
- **Test recording formats:** Do a short test to see if you can import the footage into your editing software.

- **Audio test:** Record a friend speaking and see if the levels are good. Listen for hum or interference.
- **Lighting test:** Try your lights in a space like the one you will use in your film. Practice placing them to avoid shadows or harsh spots.

If you find any problems, fix them before your shoot date. This might mean updating camera firmware or getting a new cable. Early testing can save you from panic on set.

---

## 10. Organizing and Labeling Gear

When you have multiple cameras, mics, lights, and cables, it's easy to get confused. Labeling your gear helps a lot. Use small stickers or tape:

- Mark each lens with its focal length.
- Label memory cards and their containers.
- Number your batteries so you can track which are charged and which need charging.
- Keep lights in designated cases or boxes.

Also, keep an inventory list of everything you have. This is helpful if something goes missing. You can also note the condition of the gear and check it after each shoot.

---

## 11. Protecting Your Equipment

Film equipment can be fragile and expensive. Take steps to keep it safe:

- **Use proper cases and bags:** Padding protects against knocks and drops.
- **Mind the weather:** Moisture, dust, or extreme cold/heat can damage cameras and lenses. If you're shooting outdoors, consider protective covers.
- **Stay organized on set:** Don't leave gear lying around in high-traffic areas. Use stands or tables to keep everything in one spot.
- **Insurance:** For bigger productions, consider an insurance plan that covers gear damage or theft.

## 12. Data Management and Backups

Footage is the heart of your film. Losing it can be a big setback. Develop a good routine:

1. **Offload footage after each day:** Transfer files from memory cards to at least two hard drives.
2. **Label your files:** Use scene and take numbers in file names, or keep a log.
3. **Consider cloud storage:** If you have fast internet, back up important footage online.
4. **Check footage:** Quickly review clips to ensure there were no recording errors.

Without a clear system, you might lose track of which cards have been transferred, or worse, accidentally format a card that still has valuable footage.

---

## 13. Computer and Editing Software

Your editing machine and software are part of your filmmaking tools. You don't necessarily need the most powerful computer on the market, but you do need one that can handle your footage. If you're shooting 4K video, you'll need enough RAM and a decent processor or GPU to edit smoothly. Common editing software includes:

- **Adobe Premiere Pro**
- **Final Cut Pro** (Mac only)
- **DaVinci Resolve**
- **Avid Media Composer**

Pick one you're comfortable with. You can also find free or low-cost options. Make sure you understand basic editing functions, color adjustments, and how to export a final video file.

---

## 14. Monitoring and Playback

On set, you might want a better view than the small camera screen. You can use:

- **External Monitors:** Larger displays that mount on the camera or on a stand.
- **Playback Equipment:** Allows you to review takes immediately at a bigger size, making it easier to spot focus issues or lighting flaws.

For key scenes, immediate playback helps you decide if you need another take. Just be careful not to get stuck replaying everything too often. That can slow down your shoot.

---

## 15. Special Gear for Unique Shots

Sometimes your script calls for special moves or angles. This might require unique tools:

- **Jibs or Cranes:** Let you move the camera in an arc or from high to low angles.
- **Drones:** Aerial shots can look epic, but you might need permits to fly them. Also, check local laws.
- **Underwater Housings:** If you have scenes in a pool or ocean, you need a waterproof case for your camera.
- **360 Cameras:** Capture the entire surroundings, but you must plan carefully on how to use that footage in your story.

Renting these items for a few days might be better than buying, especially if you'll only use them for one or two scenes.

---

## 16. Adapting to Your Film's Style

Every film has a certain look or tone. Your choice of gear should support that. For instance, if your film is a documentary that follows people around a busy city, you might prefer a lightweight setup with a small camera and a simple audio recorder. If your film is a carefully staged drama, you might have time to use big lights and a large camera rig on tripods or dollies. Match your tools to the demands of the script and your shooting conditions.

## 17. Budget-Friendly Tips

1. **Buy used gear:** Many professionals upgrade their gear regularly, so you can find good deals on used cameras or lenses.
2. **Look for package deals:** Rental houses sometimes offer bundles of camera, lenses, and lights at a discounted rate.
3. **Share with other filmmakers:** Splitting costs can help everyone get better gear.
4. **Use natural light:** Daylight can look great if you time your scenes well.
5. **DIY solutions:** You can build simple rigs or reflectors with affordable materials.

---

## 18. Training Your Team to Use the Tools

Having gear is one thing; using it well is another. If you have a dedicated camera operator or sound recordist, make sure they are familiar with the tools. You can do test shoots or small practice sessions before the main shoot. Talk about safety as well. Heavy lights on stands must be set up properly. Cables must be taped down. If everyone knows how to handle the gear, you reduce accidents and wasted time.

---

## 19. Respecting Time When Using Shared Equipment

If multiple departments share certain items (like a camera crane or a set of special lights), schedule who will use them and when. Time is precious on set. If the camera department hogs a piece of gear, the lighting crew might fall behind. Clear communication about who needs what tool at which moment can prevent friction.

---

## 20. Keeping a Backup Plan

Even the best gear can fail or run into problems. Have a backup plan:

- **Spare camera body or a secondary camera:** Even a decent smartphone can serve as a backup in a pinch.

- **Extra audio recorder:** If your main audio device malfunctions, you can switch to a secondary setup.
- **Multiple microphones:** Mics can break or stop working, so carry at least one extra.
- **Emergency lighting:** A few battery-powered LED lights can be a lifesaver if the power goes out or you lose your main lights.

## 21. Wireless vs. Wired Solutions

- **Wireless** mics or monitors are convenient, but they can have interference or dropouts.
- **Wired** gear can be more reliable, but you have to manage cables to avoid tripping hazards.

Think about which approach works best for your scenes. If actors need to move freely without cables, wireless might be the best choice. If they stay in one spot, wired gear might be more stable.

## 22. Audio Playback on Set for Music Scenes

If you have scenes where actors sing or dance to music, you need a way to play that music on set. A small speaker can help, but watch out for audio bleeding into your main recordings if you need clean dialogue. Usually, you film such scenes with a playback track. Then, in post-production, you replace that track with a clean version.

## 23. Checking Gear Insurance and Permits

If you rent expensive gear, the rental house might require insurance. Make sure you know what is covered in case of damage or loss. Also, if you plan to use drones or special effects, some areas require permits or special insurance. Research this early so you don't face legal or financial trouble later.

## 24. Field Monitors and LUTs

Some high-end cameras let you apply a "look-up table" (LUT) on your monitor to preview how your footage will look after color grading. This is useful if you shoot in a flat profile (like Log). Even if you are shooting on a simpler camera, you can adjust your monitor's settings to approximate your final look. This helps you see if your exposure and color are correct in real time.

---

## 25. Chapter 5 Key Points Recap

- Your choice of camera depends on your story, budget, and the look you want.
- Lenses, audio gear, and lighting kits are as important as the camera.
- Renting or borrowing gear can save money, but test everything and handle it carefully.
- Keep your gear organized, labeled, and protected from damage or theft.
- Always have a backup plan in case equipment fails.
- Plan your data storage carefully to avoid losing footage.
- Train your team on how to use the tools, and practice with test shoots.

Gathering the right tools is a major step in getting ready for production. Once you have the gear you need, you can shift your focus to shooting. In the next chapter, we will explore simple cinematography basics—how to compose your shots, move the camera, and light your scene for the best effect. This is where your camera and lighting equipment truly comes to life, transforming your script into vivid images.

---

# CHAPTER 6: SIMPLE CINEMATOGRAPHY BASICS

You have gathered your gear, and now it's time to learn how to use it effectively. Cinematography is the art of capturing images in a way that tells the story. It's not just about pointing the camera and hitting record. It's about making choices in framing, angles, movement, and lighting to guide how viewers see each scene. In this chapter, we will look at the basic concepts of cinematography in simple terms. By the end, you will know how to compose shots, follow a few fundamental guidelines, and make your visuals more engaging.

### 1. Composition: Placing Elements in the Frame

Composition is how you arrange people and objects within the frame. A well-composed shot draws the viewer's attention to what matters most. Here are some common guidelines:

1. **Rule of Thirds**
    - Imagine your frame has two vertical and two horizontal lines, dividing the image into nine boxes.
    - Place important subjects where the lines intersect. This often creates a pleasing balance.
    - This guideline is not strict, but it's a good start for framing people or objects.
2. **Headroom and Lead Room**
    - **Headroom**: The space above a person's head. Too much empty space can make the subject look small or awkward. Too little and you might cut off the top of their head.
    - **Lead Room**: If a subject is looking or moving to one side, leave some space in front of them so they don't appear cramped.
3. **Symmetry**
    - Sometimes placing a subject in the center creates a strong, balanced shot, especially in scenes with symmetrical backgrounds.
    - Symmetry can also highlight a character's loneliness if used carefully (like a single person in the middle of an empty space).

4. **Foreground, Middle Ground, Background**
    - Adding layers to your shot creates depth. You might place something in the foreground (like a lamp), the person in the middle ground, and the scenery in the background.
    - This helps the image look three-dimensional.

Experiment with composition. Walk around with your camera (or phone) and practice framing the same subject from different positions and angles. Notice how slight changes can alter the feel of the shot.

---

## 2. Camera Angles and Their Effects

Camera angles influence how the viewer perceives the subject:

1. **Eye-Level Shot**
    - The camera is at the subject's eye level.
    - Feels natural, as if the viewer is on equal footing with the character.
2. **Low Angle Shot**
    - The camera is below the subject, looking up.
    - Can make a character appear more powerful or imposing.
3. **High Angle Shot**
    - The camera is above the subject, looking down.
    - Can make a character look smaller, weaker, or in danger.
4. **Dutch Angle (Tilted Shot)**
    - The camera is tilted to create an off-balance look.
    - Often used in suspense or to show confusion.

Remember, these angles should serve the story. If your character is supposed to appear strong, a low angle might be a good choice. If you want to show them feeling vulnerable, a high angle might work better.

---

## 3. Shot Sizes

Shot size refers to how close or far the camera is from the subject:

1. **Extreme Wide Shot (EWS)**

- Shows a large area, making people or objects look small. Good for establishing location.
2. **Wide Shot (WS)**
   - Shows the subject's full body in relation to the surroundings.
3. **Medium Shot (MS)**
   - Usually frames the subject from around the waist up. Good for dialogue scenes.
4. **Close-Up (CU)**
   - Frames a subject's face or a small detail to highlight emotion or importance.
5. **Extreme Close-Up (ECU)**
   - Shows a specific part of the subject, like eyes or hands. Great for focusing on detail or heightened emotion.

Use shot sizes to control how much detail the audience sees. For intense emotional moments, a close-up reveals the actor's facial expression. For large action scenes, wide shots help the viewer understand the setting.

---

## 4. Camera Movements

Static shots can work, but adding camera moves can enhance storytelling. Here are common movements:

1. **Pan**
   - The camera turns left or right on a tripod.
   - Good for following a moving subject or revealing more of the scene.
2. **Tilt**
   - The camera looks up or down while fixed in one spot.
   - Helps show vertical movement or shift attention from one part of the scene to another.
3. **Dolly or Tracking Shot**
   - The camera moves forward, backward, or sideways on a dolly or track.
   - Often used to follow characters or move the viewer through a space.
4. **Handheld**
   - The camera is held by the operator's hands or on a shoulder rig, creating a slight shake.

- Can give a more urgent or realistic feel, often used in documentaries.
5. **Crane or Jib**
    - The camera is attached to a crane or jib, moving up and down or sweeping across a scene.
    - Good for dramatic reveals or aerial-like shots without a drone.

Use these movements with purpose. A slow push-in on a character's face can emphasize their emotion. A quick handheld shot might show chaos. Avoid random camera moves that distract the viewer.

---

## 5. The 180-Degree Rule

In a scene with two characters talking, imagine a line running between them. The 180-degree rule states that you keep the camera on one side of that line to maintain consistent screen direction. If you cross the line, the characters will appear to swap positions on screen, confusing the viewer. While you can break this rule for dramatic effect, you should understand it first.

---

## 6. Matching Shots: Continuity

Continuity means making sure details stay consistent from shot to shot. If a character is holding a cup in their right hand in one shot, they should still be holding it in their right hand in the next shot. This applies to clothing, lighting, props, and even posture. Shooting out of order is common, so you or your script supervisor should take notes or photos to ensure continuity.

---

## 7. Lighting Basics for Cinematography

Lighting can transform the mood of a scene. A few basic setups:

1. **Three-Point Lighting**
    - **Key Light:** Main light that highlights one side of the subject.
    - **Fill Light:** Softer light that reduces shadows on the opposite side.

- **Back Light:** Light placed behind the subject to separate them from the background.
2. **High-Key Lighting**
    - Bright and even with minimal shadows. Common in comedies or cheerful scenes.
3. **Low-Key Lighting**
    - Dark with strong contrasts, deep shadows. Often used in dramas or mysteries.
4. **Motivated Lighting**
    - Using practical sources in the scene (like lamps or windows) as part of your lighting strategy. This helps the lighting feel natural.

Pay attention to color temperature. Daylight is around 5600K, while tungsten lights are around 3200K, giving a warmer look. You can balance them with gels or adjust the camera's white balance to match your desired look.

---

## 8. Depth of Field

Depth of field refers to how much of the scene is in focus:

- **Shallow Depth of Field:** Only the subject is in clear focus, while the background and foreground are blurred. This can draw attention to the subject.
- **Deep Depth of Field:** Much of the frame is in focus, which can be useful for scenes where you want the viewer to see the environment.

Choosing your aperture and the distance between the camera, subject, and background affects depth of field. Use it to guide the viewer's eye to what is important in the shot.

---

## 9. Color and Mood

Color choices can communicate emotion. Even if you aren't doing heavy color grading later, you can pick certain color palettes for costumes, sets, or lighting gels. Cool tones (blues and greens) might feel calm or tense, while warm tones (reds and oranges) can feel cozy or intense. Consistency in color across scenes helps the film feel unified.

## 10. Framing Characters in Dialogue Scenes

When two characters talk, you can use:

- **Over-the-Shoulder Shots:** Camera over one person's shoulder, focusing on the other person's face. This adds depth and keeps both in the scene.
- **Reverse Angles:** For the other character's perspective, you place the camera on the opposite side.
- **Two-Shot:** Both characters in one frame, often used for comedic or partner scenes.

Decide which approach fits your scene's mood. Over-the-shoulder shots are common for serious talks. A two-shot might work for a relaxed or humorous moment.

---

## 11. Shooting for Editing

As you capture scenes, think about how they will cut together in the edit. Get enough coverage: wide shots, medium shots, close-ups, inserts of important details. This gives the editor options later. If a performance is weak in the wide shot, you might rely on a close-up. If you're missing a close-up of a key prop, the scene may feel incomplete.

---

## 12. Working with Natural Light

Shooting outdoors can be beautiful but unpredictable. The sun moves, weather changes, and clouds can alter your lighting. Plan around:

- **Golden Hour:** Short period just after sunrise or before sunset. The sun is low, creating soft, warm light.
- **Midday Sun:** Harsh overhead light can create strong shadows. You might need diffusers or reflectors.
- **Cloudy Days:** The sky acts like a giant diffuser, giving soft, even light, but colors might look dull.

If you rely on natural light, know the sunrise and sunset times for your location. Move quickly to capture shots during the best light.

## 13. Using Reflectors and Diffusers

You don't need expensive lights to shape sunlight. A simple reflector can bounce light back onto your subject, filling in shadows. A diffuser can soften harsh sunlight. These are affordable tools that can drastically improve the look of outdoor or window-lit scenes.

---

## 14. Monitoring Your Shots

Whenever possible, use an external monitor or at least a viewfinder that shows accurate color and exposure. The small screen on your camera might not always give a clear idea of how bright or dark your footage is. Check the histogram or waveform if your camera has it. If everything is too bright (clipped highlights) or too dark (crushed blacks), adjust your aperture, ISO, or lighting to fix it.

---

## 15. Storyboarding for Cinematography

Storyboarding is drawing out your shots beforehand. Even simple sketches can help you plan composition, angles, and camera moves. You don't have to be an artist. Stick figures and arrows are enough if they show the shot layout. This saves time on set because you have a roadmap of how you want each scene to look.

---

## 16. Blocking Actors

Blocking refers to how actors move in a scene. As you block the scene, consider:

- Where they enter or exit.
- When they change position to show a shift in mood or focus.
- How they interact with objects or furniture.

You then decide where the camera goes to capture these movements. Rehearse blocking with the actors so they know their marks. This helps you set up the camera angles and lights without confusion.

## 17. Handling Movement Scenes

Action scenes or scenes with a lot of movement can be tricky. Plan them in stages:

- **Mark the path** the actors will take.
- **Choose a camera move** that follows or anticipates the movement.
- **Check safety** if the scene involves running or stunts.
- **Rehearse** multiple times to avoid missed focus or shaky framing.

You can use slow motion for dramatic effect, but remember you need more light if you shoot at higher frame rates.

## 18. Keeping Shots Steady

Shaky shots can be distracting unless the scene calls for a frantic vibe. Use a tripod or stabilizer if you need smooth footage. If you have to go handheld, practice holding the camera close to your body. Bend your knees slightly. Avoid sudden jerks. A little controlled sway can look more organic than random shaking.

## 19. Camera Settings to Remember

- **Shutter Speed:** Generally, for cinematic motion blur, use the 180-degree shutter rule. If you shoot at 24fps, use about 1/48 sec shutter speed.
- **ISO:** Keep it as low as possible for cleaner images. If it's too dark, add light instead of cranking ISO (if you can).
- **Aperture (f-stop):** Controls depth of field and exposure.
- **White Balance:** Match your lighting source. If you are outdoors, pick daylight. If indoors with tungsten, pick a warmer setting.
- **Picture Profile or Log:** Some cameras let you record a flat image (Log) for more control in color grading. That can require extra time in post-production.

## 20. Using Camera Filters

Filters can help you control the light or add effects:

- **Neutral Density (ND) Filters:** Reduce the amount of light entering the lens. Useful for keeping a shallow depth of field in bright sunlight.
- **Polarizing Filters:** Cut reflections and boost colors in the sky.
- **Soft or Pro-Mist Filters:** Can give a slight glow to highlights, often used to soften skin tones.

Test these filters beforehand to avoid surprises with color shifts or vignettes.

---

## 21. Practice Shots Before the Real Take

If you have time, do a quick rehearsal with the camera rolling. Watch it back to see if the framing, focus, and movement look good. This is especially important for complex moves or crane shots. A short run-through can reveal issues like harsh shadows on the actor's face or a shaky camera move.

---

## 22. Visual Storytelling

Remember that every shot should contribute to the story. Ask yourself: "Does this angle or movement help show the character's emotions or the tension in the scene?" Avoid flashy camera moves that don't serve a purpose. Simple can be powerful if it fits the mood of the scene.

---

## 23. Keeping an Eye on the Background

It's easy to focus on the actors and forget the background. Look out for distracting elements like a bright window, a messy object, or a random stranger in the distance. Adjust your camera angle or depth of field to keep the background clean or relevant.

---

## 24. Getting Creative

Once you master the basics, you can try more artistic shots. Maybe tilt the camera slightly for a sense of unease. Maybe place an actor in a corner of the frame to show isolation. As long as it fits the story, creativity is encouraged. But always remember the main goal: help the audience connect with what's happening on screen.

---

## 25. Chapter 6 Key Points Recap

- Composition, angles, and shot sizes shape the viewer's experience.
- Camera movement should serve the story, not distract from it.
- Follow the 180-degree rule to keep characters' positions clear.
- Lighting choices (high-key, low-key, three-point) affect mood.
- Always consider color, depth of field, and continuity.
- Plan shots with storyboards and block actors to match the camera plan.
- Pay attention to camera settings, filters, and gear to get the best image possible.
- Keep the background in mind and practice with test shots to avoid surprises.

With these simple cinematography basics, you are ready to bring your script to life in a clear, visually appealing way. The next stage is to explore more advanced camera techniques and specialized methods that can give your film a distinct style. By building on this foundation, you will learn how to handle tricky lighting situations, dynamic camera moves, and other challenges. In the upcoming chapters, we will continue to grow your skills so you can shoot your film with confidence.

# CHAPTER 7: ADVANCED CAMERA TECHNIQUES

You have learned simple cinematography basics. Now it's time to build on those skills with advanced camera techniques. These methods go beyond basic framing and movement. They let you handle tricky shooting conditions, add extra style, and get smoother or more unique shots. In this chapter, we will look at specialized moves, focus methods, camera rigs, multi-camera setups, and other ideas that can make your movie look more polished. We will keep things easy to understand, but we will cover enough detail so you can try these techniques on your own shoot.

## 1. Complex Camera Moves

Simple pans and tilts are common. But there are more complex moves that can draw the audience into your story:

1. **Dolly Zoom (also known as the "Vertigo Shot")**
   - This involves moving the camera forward or backward while zooming the lens in the opposite direction.
   - The background size appears to change while the subject stays the same size in the frame.
   - It creates a strange feeling, often used to show a character's sudden realization or anxiety.
2. **Arc Shot**
   - The camera moves in a curved path around a subject or group of subjects.
   - This can reveal different angles of a character's face or the setting.
   - It adds energy to a scene, especially during important conversations or emotional moments.
3. **Whip Pan**
   - A fast, blurry pan from one subject to another.
   - Often used for comedic transitions or to connect two scenes quickly.
   - You need to practice so you don't lose your subject or end up with confusing motion blur.

Practice these moves with test footage before you use them on a real shoot. For a dolly zoom, you need a lens that can zoom smoothly and a dolly or slider that keeps camera movement consistent. For an arc shot, plan where the track or path will be, making sure you avoid obstacles. For a whip pan, rehearse your speed so the camera lands on the new subject in focus.

## 2. Advanced Focusing Methods

Keeping your subject sharp is essential. Sometimes, basic auto-focus or manual focus might not be enough. Here are a few methods to achieve better results:

1. **Pull Focus (or Rack Focus)**
   - You shift focus from one subject to another in the same shot.
   - For example, you start focused on a character in the background, then smoothly move the focus to a character in the foreground.
   - This guides the viewer's eye without cutting to a different shot.
2. **Follow Focus**
   - You keep a moving subject in focus as it or the camera moves.
   - Often used in action scenes or when an actor walks toward the camera.
   - You can use special follow focus wheels on the camera rig for smoother control.
3. **Zone Focusing**
   - You set a certain depth of field range in which the subject will remain sharp.
   - This is handy for scenes where you can't manually focus fast enough (like fast-moving crowds).
   - You pick an aperture that gives enough depth of field to keep the main action area in focus.

You might want a camera assistant whose main job is to pull focus. On larger sets, this person works with marks on the floor that indicate where an actor will stand. They measure the distance and adjust focus rings precisely. If you're working on a smaller set without an extra person, plan your shots so that focus changes are simpler (for instance, less movement or a deeper depth of field).

## 3. High-Speed and Slow-Motion Shots

**High-speed** filming means shooting at a higher frame rate than normal. For instance, if you shoot at 60 frames per second (fps) but play back at 24 fps, the footage appears to move slower. This can add drama to a scene, such as an object falling or a character reacting in shock.

- **Check your camera's capabilities:** Some cameras can shoot 120 fps or higher, but they may need strong lighting.
- **Watch your shutter speed:** A general rule is to use a shutter speed that is about double the frame rate. If you shoot at 60 fps, a shutter of around 1/120 second can give a natural look.
- **Be mindful of storage:** High frame rates create larger files, so bring enough memory cards or hard drives.

**Time-lapse** is the opposite idea. You record fewer frames over a long period, then play them back at normal speed. This can show clouds racing across the sky or traffic rushing through a city. It works well for transitions or to show the passage of time.

---

## 4. Working with Gimbals and Stabilizers

Handheld shots can add excitement, but too much shaking is distracting. Gimbals and other stabilizers help you get smooth footage while moving:

1. **3-Axis Gimbal**
    - An electronic device that uses motors to keep the camera stable on three axes (tilt, roll, and pan).
    - You hold the gimbal with both hands, and as you walk, the camera remains level.
    - Great for tracking shots following actors, or for fluid movements in tight spaces.
2. **Steadicam**
    - A mechanical stabilizer worn by an operator with a vest and an arm.
    - It balances the camera's weight so the operator can walk or run while keeping the footage stable.
    - Requires training to use well, but it's common in professional films.
3. **Shoulder Rig**

- Not fully stabilized like a gimbal, but it reduces some shake by mounting the camera on your shoulder.
- Helps you shoot for longer without arm strain.
- Works well for documentary or "run-and-gun" style filming.

Practice with these tools. Walk around, try corners or stairs, and learn how quickly you can pan or tilt. Each stabilizer has its own limits. The better you know your equipment, the more confidently you can plan camera moves during the shoot.

---

## 5. Drone Cinematography

Drones allow you to capture aerial shots without renting a helicopter. They can give your film a high-budget feel. However, drones also come with rules:

1. **Legal Permits:** Many places require special permission or licenses to fly drones, especially if you plan to use the footage commercially.
2. **Safety:** You must be careful about people, buildings, and power lines.
3. **Battery Life:** Drone batteries don't last very long (often 20–30 minutes), so plan your shots carefully.
4. **Wind and Weather:** Wind can shake the drone, causing unstable footage. Rain can damage it.

If you want a big, sweeping shot of a landscape, a drone is a great option. Just practice flying in a safe area first. Also, set your camera settings for stable results. Many drones have built-in gimbals for smooth footage. Keep an eye on your frame rate, shutter speed, and exposure. Also note that drone footage often looks best when combined with ground-level shots, so the aerial shots don't feel random.

---

## 6. Using Sliders and Dollies

We touched on basic dollies before, but let's explore more details:

1. **Sliders**
   - A small track, usually 1–3 feet long. You put the camera on a sliding plate and move it left-to-right or forward-back.

- Ideal for subtle camera moves that add life to a static shot.
- Easy to set up compared to a full dolly track.
2. **Doorway Dolly**
   - A simple dolly with wheels, named because it can fit through a doorway.
   - You can attach a seat for the operator or just place the tripod on it.
   - Good for tracking shots indoors.
3. **Track Dolly**
   - A heavier system that runs on rails.
   - Provides very smooth movement over a greater distance.
   - Requires time to set up tracks on level ground.

Plan your path in advance. If you need a shot that slowly moves closer to a character, you can place the slider in front of them and decide how long the move should take. Rehearse to find the right speed. A well-done slider or dolly shot can focus attention or reveal important details.

---

## 7. Multi-Camera Shooting

Most small films use one camera. But sometimes, you can use two or more cameras at once. This can save time and offer more angles:

1. **Live Events or Performances**
   - You can capture the wide shot with one camera and close-ups with another.
   - This is common in concerts or stage shows.
2. **Action Scenes**
   - Having more cameras means you can get different angles of stunts or explosions without needing the action repeated many times (which can be expensive or unsafe).
3. **Interviews or Dialogue**
   - You can film both actors simultaneously with two cameras. This helps keep performances consistent. You don't have to redo lines to capture the other angle.

When you edit multi-camera footage, sync the clips using a slate or timecode. This helps you quickly cut between cameras. Make sure each camera has a similar color profile and settings, or you might have trouble matching the shots in post.

## 8. Underwater and Special Enclosures

If your film has water scenes, you might need special cases:

- **Underwater Housing:** A sealed case around your camera. Good for underwater shots in a pool, lake, or ocean.
- **Splash Bags:** Less sturdy but cheaper than full housings. They protect your camera from splashes or rain but may not allow you to fully submerge the camera.

You also need to consider lighting underwater. Water blocks light quickly, so you may need waterproof lights or plan your shoot when the sunlight is bright and the water is clear. Safety is key: do test runs without your main camera to see if everything works well.

## 9. Working with Green Screen or Blue Screen

Sometimes you need a background or location you can't have in real life. That's where green screens help. You shoot the actor against a green backdrop, then replace the green with a different background in post-production. Key tips:

1. **Even Lighting:** Make sure the green screen is lit evenly. Shadows or hot spots can cause problems when you remove the green.
2. **Distance from Background:** Place the subject a few feet away from the screen to avoid green spill on their clothes or skin.
3. **High-Quality Footage:** If your camera compresses the video too much, you may see blocky edges. A camera that records at a higher bit rate makes keying easier.

Plan your final background so you know how to match the camera angle and lighting. If the background is supposed to be a sunny beach, you might light the subject in a warm, bright way. If it's a dark forest, tone down the lighting to match the mood.

## 10. Bullet Time and Advanced Rigs

"Bullet time" became famous from scenes that freeze action while the camera moves around the subject. It typically involves many cameras placed in a circle or arc, all triggering at the same moment. This is quite complicated and might be out of reach for most beginner projects, but it's worth noting:

- You need multiple cameras of the same model and lens, arranged carefully.
- You need a system to trigger all the shutters at once.
- You need lots of space and a method to store all that footage.

This technique is more common in big-budget films or high-end commercials. If you have access to a film school or a studio with such a setup, you could try it for a special effect. Otherwise, simpler advanced methods (like a single camera on a track with high-speed shooting) might be enough to show slow-motion or a dramatic effect.

---

## 11. Camera Filters for Specific Looks

We discussed ND filters and polarizers before, but advanced shooters sometimes use other filters:

1. **Split Diopter:** Allows part of the frame to be focused at one distance, and another part at a different distance. You see this in scenes where a face in the foreground is sharp, and an object in the background is also sharp, with a blurry band in the middle.
2. **Color Filters or Gels:** Attach them in front of the lens to create a colored tint. More common in older films, but can be used today for artistic style.
3. **Infrared (IR) Filters:** Capture infrared light for a surreal or scientific look. This is quite specialized.

As always, test these filters. They can create unique visual styles but might also complicate your lighting or focus.

## 12. Advanced Framing Tricks

Beyond the rule of thirds, you can use:

1. **Leading Lines:** Use lines in the environment (roads, fences, hallways) that direct the viewer's eyes to the subject.
2. **Frame within a Frame:** Place your subject inside a doorway, window, or any shape that frames them. This draws attention and adds depth.
3. **Negative Space:** Leave empty space around the subject to make them stand out or to show loneliness.

These tricks can elevate the visual impact of a scene. Watch classic films or photography for examples of creative framing.

---

## 13. Mixing Handheld and Locked-Off Shots

Some directors like the raw, realistic feel of handheld shots for certain moments, and stable, locked-off shots for calmer moments. Switching between these styles can communicate mood changes. For example, you might have a smooth dolly shot in a quiet scene, then jump to a shaky handheld shot during an argument or chase.

---

## 14. Coordinating with the Editing Plan

Advanced camera techniques are fun, but always remember how these shots will fit into the edit. If you plan a complex crane shot that ends with a top-down view, make sure you know what shot will come right before and after it. You might need a matching angle or a cutaway to keep continuity.

---

## 15. Team Coordination for Complex Shots

Some moves require more crew members:

- **Crane Shots:** You might need a dedicated crane operator and a grip to balance it.

- **Focus Pull:** A camera assistant stands by with a follow focus wheel, adjusting focus based on marks.
- **Dolly and Boom:** You might have one person pushing the dolly while another handles the camera's tilt.

Have a short rehearsal. Mark any important points on the floor with tape. Use verbal cues during the shot. For instance, the director or assistant director might say, "Dolly in… now," so the dolly grip knows when to start moving.

---

## 16. Night Shooting and Exposure Challenges

Night shoots can be tricky. Advanced techniques to handle low light:

1. **Fast Lenses (Low f-stop):** This lets in more light and allows shooting in darker conditions.
2. **High ISO Performance:** Some cameras are good at high ISOs with less noise, but you must do tests to see how far you can push them before the image becomes grainy.
3. **Practical Lights:** Street lamps or store signs can be used as part of your lighting. If you add small hidden lights or reflectors, you might get enough illumination to keep the scene clear.
4. **Car Scenes:** You can use small LED panels inside the car or reflect street lights. Large studio shoots often rig big lights on process trailers, but you might have to be creative with smaller gear.

Always do a quick playback on set to see if the footage is too dark. Shooting at night can be time-consuming, so plan carefully.

---

## 17. Handling Extreme Conditions

What if your script calls for filming in a desert or a snowy mountain?

- **Protect Your Gear:** In sandy areas, use covers or tape to block dust. In cold climates, keep batteries warm, as they drain faster in the cold.
- **Check Weather:** A sudden storm can ruin your shot plan.
- **Stay Safe:** Bring enough water, proper clothing, and emergency supplies.

Advanced camera techniques can help you capture striking visuals in these places. For example, a slow-motion shot of blowing sand can look impressive, or a wide drone shot over a snowfield can set a dramatic scene. Just make sure you and your crew are prepared.

---

## 18. Shooting Action Scenes Safely

Action scenes involve movement, stunts, or special effects. You might use advanced camera work like quick pans, handheld chaos, or multiple cameras. Key safety tips:

- **Plan Stunts in Detail:** Use stunt coordinators if possible.
- **Mark Safe Zones:** Keep the camera team out of the path of vehicles, fights, or pyrotechnics.
- **Rehearse at Half-Speed:** Let everyone see how the scene will unfold before doing it at full speed.
- **Protect Equipment:** Shield cameras from debris or fire with covers or distance.

Action scenes can be the highlight of your film, but you don't want injuries or damaged gear. Plan thoroughly and do test runs.

---

## 19. Creative Transitions In-Camera

Sometimes you can create transitions without relying on editing effects:

1. **Match Cut in Camera:** End a shot on an object with a certain shape or motion, then start the next shot with a similar shape or motion. For example, someone slams a door, and in the next shot, a box is slammed down.
2. **Wipe with a Person or Object:** Pan the camera so an object (like a wall or a person's back) briefly fills the screen. Then start the next shot with that same color or shape.
3. **Zoom In and Out Transitions:** Zoom in on a subject until it's almost black, then in the next scene, zoom out from a dark area.

These transitions keep the film flowing in a clever way and can add interest. Practice them to avoid jumpy or awkward cuts.

## 20. Pre-Visualization and Virtual Tools

Large productions use pre-visualization software or 3D models to plan complicated camera moves. Even if you're working on a smaller film, you can try basic storyboarding apps or free 3D tools to map out your shots. This can save time on set and help you spot problems (like blocked camera paths) in advance.

---

## 21. Mixing Old and New Tech

There is a trend where some filmmakers mix modern digital cameras with old lenses or even old analog cameras. This can add a distinct look with unique color and sharpness differences. You can also experiment with old film stocks if your budget allows. Just remember that you need labs to develop physical film, and you must handle film carefully on set. If you only have digital gear, you can simulate old film looks in post-production with color grading or film grain overlays, but real vintage gear can be a fun approach if you know how to handle it.

---

## 22. Monitoring Advanced Shots

When performing advanced techniques, an external monitor or video village (a separate station with a larger screen) can be helpful. The director, cinematographer, and other key crew can watch the shot as it happens. This is especially important for:

- Dolly or crane moves, where you can't see the camera screen easily.
- Multi-camera setups, so you can monitor each camera's angle.
- Green screen shots, to ensure the subject is framed correctly and no green spills on them.

A good monitor helps you catch small mistakes, like an out-of-focus face or a microphone dipping into the frame.

---

## 23. Keeping Things Organized

Advanced techniques often mean more gear: extra cameras, rigs, cables, or remote controls. You need to label everything and keep it tidy to avoid confusion. Also, keep a shot list or breakdown of which advanced moves happen in which scenes. This helps you avoid missing any planned shots, especially if time is tight.

## 24. Improving Through Practice

Advanced camera work takes practice. If you rarely attempt a dolly zoom, it might look rough the first time. Don't wait for the big shooting day to try it. Do small test shoots in your backyard or a local park. Watch tutorials. Learn from any mistakes. This practice helps you feel comfortable on set, where time is money.

## 25. Chapter 7 Key Points Recap

- Complex camera moves like dolly zooms, arc shots, and whip pans can add impact to your storytelling.
- Advanced focusing methods (pull focus, follow focus) let you direct attention without cutting.
- Gimbals, Steadicams, drones, and dollies help you get smooth or dramatic movements.
- Multi-camera setups save time or capture multiple angles at once.
- Green screen and underwater filming require careful lighting and planning.
- Practice advanced rigs or shots before shooting day, and keep safety a top priority.
- A good external monitor and shot planning tools will help you spot problems early.
- Organize your gear and your shot list to avoid confusion.

With these advanced camera techniques, you can add excitement and style to your film. Next, in Chapter 8, we move on to lighting basics and methods. We will look at core lighting principles, gear choices, and ways to shape and control light. A strong understanding of lighting—both indoors and outdoors—is essential for a professional-looking movie. Let's keep building your skills so you can create images that truly support your story.

# CHAPTER 8: LIGHTING BASICS AND METHODS

Lighting is a major part of filmmaking. It helps set the mood, draws attention to key parts of the scene, and shapes the overall look of your movie. Even if you have a great camera and lens, poor lighting can make your film look amateurish. Fortunately, you don't need the most expensive lights to achieve a strong result. You just need to understand how light works and how to use it effectively. In this chapter, we will discuss different types of lights, how to set them up, simple lighting styles, and how to adapt to various locations. By the end, you will be ready to light your scenes with confidence.

## 1. The Purpose of Good Lighting

Before we look at specific techniques, let's be clear about why lighting matters:

1. **Visibility:** Obviously, you want the audience to see the actors and important details.
2. **Mood:** Bright, even light can feel cheerful. Dark, shadowy light can feel tense or mysterious.
3. **Depth:** Proper lighting can separate the subject from the background, giving the image a sense of space.
4. **Focus:** You can light certain areas more strongly, guiding the audience's eye to what is important.

Your script and story will guide the lighting style. A comedy might use bright, even lighting, while a thriller might use more shadow and contrast. Keep this in mind as you pick your lights and plan your setups.

## 2. Common Types of Film Lights

Modern filmmakers have several types of lights available, each with pros and cons:

1. **LED Panels**
   - Popular for their cool operation (they don't get too hot) and energy efficiency.
   - Often dimmable, with an option to change color temperature from daylight to tungsten.
   - Lightweight and easy to move around.
2. **Tungsten Lights**
   - Traditional, warm-toned lights (around 3200K).
   - Can reach high wattages (like 1,000W or more) to produce bright outputs.
   - They get hot and use more power, so watch out for heat and handle them carefully.
3. **HMI Lights**
   - Very bright, daylight-balanced lights.
   - Used for larger sets or outdoor shoots where you need a strong punch to match sunlight.
   - They can be expensive and might need special power requirements.
4. **Florescent or Soft Lights**
   - Provide a diffused, soft glow.
   - Good for interviews or close-up work where you need gentle, even illumination.
   - Flickering can be an issue if you use mismatched lights or certain camera shutter speeds.
5. **Practical Lights**
   - Lamps, overhead bulbs, candles, or any light source that actually appears in the scene.
   - Often used in combination with your film lights to make the scene feel natural.

No single type of light is "best" for all situations. You pick based on your budget, the scene's needs, and the look you want.

---

## 3. Three-Point Lighting

A classic lighting setup for many scenes or interviews is the three-point method. It includes:

1. **Key Light**

- The main source of illumination.
- Placed slightly to one side of the camera, aiming at the subject's face.
- Decides how your subject is primarily lit.
2. **Fill Light**
    - A softer light that fills in the shadows created by the key light.
    - Placed on the opposite side of the key, usually at a lower intensity.
    - Controls the contrast level.
3. **Back Light (or Rim Light)**
    - Positioned behind the subject, often high up, to create a highlight on their hair or shoulders.
    - Helps separate the subject from the background.

While three-point lighting is a great foundation, you don't need to stick to it exactly. Sometimes you'll skip the fill if you want a dramatic, high-contrast look. Or you might add extra lights to illuminate the background. However, three-point is a handy starting point when you're unsure how to begin.

---

## 4. High-Key vs. Low-Key Lighting

- **High-Key Lighting**
    - Bright, even, minimal shadows.
    - Used in comedies, commercials, or happy scenes.
    - The fill light is almost as strong as the key light, reducing contrast.
- **Low-Key Lighting**
    - Dark, strong contrast, with deep shadows.
    - Common in film noir, horror, or dramatic scenes.
    - The fill light is weak or absent, letting shadows dominate.

Decide which approach fits your scene's mood. A cheerful daytime living-room scene might have high-key lighting. A tense interrogation scene might go for a low-key style, with a single overhead lamp casting dark shadows on the character's face.

---

## 5. Color Temperature and White Balance

**Color temperature** is measured in Kelvin (K). Daylight is around 5600K (blueish), while tungsten is about 3200K (warmer). Your camera's white balance must match the main light source. If you are shooting in daylight but your camera is set to tungsten, the footage will look very blue. If your lights are mixed (part tungsten, part daylight), you can use gels or filters to match their color or create a blend of colors for dramatic effect.

---

## 6. Light Modifiers

A raw light source can be harsh, creating strong shadows. You can soften or shape the light using:

1. **Softboxes:** Attach to lights to spread them out, reducing harshness.
2. **Umbrellas:** Also soften the beam, often used in photography and some film sets.
3. **Diffusers or Silks:** Sheets of translucent material you place between the light and the subject.
4. **Flags or Cutters:** Solid panels that block part of the light to create shadows or keep light from spilling onto areas you want dark.
5. **Barn Doors:** Metal flaps on the light itself. You can adjust them to control where the light falls.

Experiment with these modifiers to see how they affect the look. A simple LED panel with a diffuser can create a pleasing glow on someone's face without harsh shadows.

---

## 7. Reflectors and Bouncing Light

Bouncing light off a white wall, a piece of foam board, or a special reflector can give you a soft fill. This is cheaper and easier than adding a second light. For instance, if you have a single strong source on one side of the actor, place a bounce card on the other side to reflect some of that light back onto their face. Reflectors come in different colors—silver, gold, or white—each adding a slightly different tone.

## 8. Practical Lighting on Set

If your scene is in a living room, you might have a lamp on a table or overhead lights. These real lights are called practicals. You can use them in combination with your film lights. For example, you might put a stronger bulb in the table lamp so it adds more light. You can also place a small LED hidden behind that lamp to boost the effect. The goal is for the audience to think the lamp is lighting the room, but you're really supplementing it with your own hidden lights.

## 9. Lighting Exterior Day Scenes

You might wonder, "Why do I need lights outside in daylight?" Sometimes the sun is very bright, creating hard shadows under the eyes. You can use reflectors or fill lights to balance it. Key tips for outdoor daylight:

1. **Use the Sun as a Key Light:** Position your subject so that the sun hits from the side or at an angle, rather than straight overhead.
2. **Fill with a Reflector:** If one side of the face is too dark, bounce some sunlight onto it.
3. **Consider Time of Day:** Early morning or late afternoon light is softer and more golden. Midday sun can be harsh and overhead.

If your budget is larger, you could bring HMI lights or strong LED panels to fill in shadows. But for many indie films, reflectors and good positioning can do the job.

## 10. Lighting Exterior Night Scenes

Night exteriors can be challenging because everything is dark. You can use street lights, store signs, or car headlights as part of the setting. But usually, you need some additional lights:

1. **Moonlight Effect:** If you want a gentle bluish tone to mimic moonlight, you can use a large HMI or daylight-balanced LED with a slight blue gel, placed high up.

2. **Practical Street Lamps:** You could replace bulbs in a real street lamp with a higher watt version if allowed. Check permits.
3. **Small LED Panels or Battery-Powered Lights:** Hide them behind objects, to simulate light from windows or doorways.

The key is to make sure your characters are visible enough to see their faces. Often, night scenes in movies are not as dark as real life. The audience needs to see what's happening while still feeling it's nighttime.

---

## 11. Motivated Lighting

"Motivated lighting" means the source of your scene's light makes sense within the story. For instance, if it's supposed to be a cozy living room, your main light could be motivated by a lamp or fireplace. You then place your actual film light in a position that seems logical for that lamp, even if it's bigger or stronger. This keeps the audience immersed.

---

## 12. Controlling Contrast

Contrast is the difference between the brightest and darkest areas. You can control it with fill lights, reflectors, or choosing a camera setting that captures a broad range. High contrast can look dramatic but might lose detail in shadows or highlights. Low contrast keeps more detail but can look flat if overdone. Test your lighting ratio—a comparison of key vs. fill brightness—to see what fits the scene.

---

## 13. Different Looks with Gels and Colors

Colored gels let you shift the color of your light:

- **Blue Gel (CTB):** Converts tungsten light (warm) to daylight (cool).
- **Orange Gel (CTO):** Converts daylight-balanced lights (cool) to a warmer tungsten look.
- **Colored Gels (Red, Green, Purple, etc.):** Useful for club scenes, fantasy moods, or stylized effects.

Experiment carefully. Sometimes a slight color tint can set a mood without distracting the viewer. But bright, unnatural colors can be used for dream sequences or music videos. Always check your camera's white balance if mixing color temperatures.

## 14. Lighting for Different Skin Tones

People have different skin tones, which can reflect light differently. Test your lighting on the actual actors if you can. You might find that one actor needs a softer light or a slightly warmer fill to avoid looking washed out. In group scenes with varied skin tones, balance your lighting so that everyone looks good on camera. One method is to use a neutral key light, then subtle fill adjustments for each side if needed.

## 15. Working in Tight Spaces

Shooting in a small room can be tough if you have big lights or lots of stands. You may need to:

1. **Use Smaller LED Panels:** They're easier to tuck into corners or attach to walls.
2. **Bounce off Walls:** White walls can become large soft sources of light.
3. **Clip Lights:** Small fixtures you can clip to door frames or shelves.
4. **Move Furniture:** Create space for your stands, but keep the set looking consistent.

Careful planning and creative use of reflectors can help you avoid an overcrowded set.

## 16. Chiaroscuro Lighting

Chiaroscuro is a classic style where you use strong contrasts of light and shadow. Think of film noir detective scenes with slanted light through blinds. You might use a single bright source angled so that part of the face is lit and the rest is in deep shadow. To achieve this:

- Turn off other lights that might fill in shadows.
- Use a focused beam (like a Fresnel light) or barn doors to shape the light.
- Position the actor so the shadows fall dramatically across their face or the background.

This style can add mystery or tension to a scene. But be careful—if the audience can't see the actor's expression at all, you might lose the emotional impact.

---

## 17. Candlelight Scenes

If your story has a scene lit by candles or a fireplace, you can do it two ways:

1. **Actual Candlelight:** Cameras today can sometimes handle low-light if you use fast lenses and high ISO settings. But it might still be too dark or noisy. You could also place reflective materials around the set to bounce candlelight.
2. **Fake Candlelight:** Use small LED lights or bulbs hidden behind candles. They flicker a bit to mimic a real flame. You can also wave your hand or a piece of cloth near the light to create a subtle flicker effect.

Do tests to see if you have enough exposure. Candlelit scenes look lovely if done well, but they can be hard to expose properly.

---

## 18. Large Set or Green Screen Lighting

If your set is large or you're lighting a green screen, you need bigger lights or more lights:

1. **Even Lighting on the Green Screen:** Avoid hot spots or wrinkles that cause uneven color.
2. **Separate the Subject:** Light the actor separately from the screen if possible, so green doesn't spill onto them.
3. **High Ceilings or Large Spaces:** You might rig lights overhead or bring in big stands. A location scout helps you plan these setups.

For big sets, a lighting plan or diagram is often made beforehand, showing where each light goes and what its purpose is.

## 19. Light Meters and False Color

Some cinematographers use a light meter to measure the exact light level. This helps maintain consistent exposure across shots. If your camera has a "false color" or "zebra stripes" function, you can see which parts of the image are overexposed or underexposed. This is extremely helpful when setting lights. By knowing where your highlights and shadows fall, you can fine-tune your setup to avoid blowing out bright areas or losing detail in shadows.

## 20. Adapting on the Fly

Even if you plan carefully, real sets and conditions might force you to change your lighting setup. Maybe you lose some gear or the sun sets faster than expected. Learn to improvise:

- Use available lights (like household lamps) in creative ways.
- Move your key light to a different angle if the location's layout changes.
- If you're outdoors and it's now dark, can you incorporate a street lamp or car headlights?

Staying calm and flexible is part of being a good filmmaker.

## 21. Safety Tips

Lights can be hot (especially tungsten) and draw a lot of power. Follow basic rules:

- **Avoid Overloading Circuits:** Check how many watts your lights use. Spread them across outlets if needed.
- **Keep Flammable Items Away:** Curtains, paper, or cloth can catch fire if they touch hot lights.
- **Secure Stands:** Use sandbags so lights don't tip over and injure someone.
- **Watch for Cables:** Tape them to the floor or route them safely so nobody trips.

A safe set is a productive set.

## 22. Maintaining Continuity in Lighting

If you shoot a scene over multiple days, you must keep the lighting consistent. Take photos or notes of your setup. Mark stand positions on the floor with tape. If something moves, you can refer to these notes to recreate the same look. This is especially important for scenes that are supposed to happen in a single timeline moment but are shot over several days.

---

## 23. Working with a Small Lighting Kit

If your budget is tiny, consider:

- Using practicals and buying brighter bulbs that match your camera's white balance.
- Borrowing or renting a couple of LED panels.
- Using cheap reflectors or foam boards from a craft store to bounce light.
- Shooting near windows when it's daylight.

You can still get a professional look by being creative with the few lights you have. The script and the mood should guide your choices, not just the number of lights.

---

## 24. Testing and Tweaking

Always do a camera test with your lighting before rolling on the real take. Look at the monitor or do a quick playback. Check:

- Are there weird shadows on the actor's face?
- Is the background too dark or too bright?
- Does the lighting color match the scene's mood?

Sometimes just a slight angle adjustment or adding a small bounce card can fix an issue. Five minutes of testing can save you from bad footage.

## 25. Chapter 8 Key Points Recap

- Lighting sets the scene's mood and helps the audience see what's important.
- You can use different types of lights: LED, tungsten, HMI, fluorescent, or practicals.
- Three-point lighting is a great starting method, but you can adapt it to your needs.
- High-key lighting is bright and cheerful; low-key lighting is dark and dramatic.
- Reflectors, diffusers, and other modifiers help you shape the light.
- Match color temperatures and use gels to blend or stylize light sources.
- Outdoor shoots still need lighting control, especially for harsh or low light.
- Large sets might need bigger or multiple lights, while small rooms need clever positioning.
- Keep your set safe, watch continuity, and test everything before you shoot.

With this knowledge of lighting basics and methods, you can shape the look of your film. Even if you have limited equipment, using these ideas will elevate your images. Next, in Chapter 9, we explore capturing sound on set. Good sound is just as important as good visuals, and we will look at microphones, techniques to reduce unwanted noise, and ways to ensure your dialogue is crisp. By combining strong lighting with clear audio, you'll be well on your way to a professional-looking (and sounding) film.

# CHAPTER 9: CAPTURING SOUND ON SET

When people watch a movie, they usually pay attention to what they see on screen. But sound is just as important. In fact, viewers often notice poor sound more than a slightly blurry shot. If your dialogue is unclear or your soundtrack is full of unwanted noise, the overall quality of your film suffers. This chapter teaches you how to record sound on set so it's clear, consistent, and easy to work with during post-production. We will explore different microphones, recording devices, best practices for location sound, and tips to avoid common pitfalls. By the end, you should have a solid plan for capturing audio for your film.

## 1. Why Sound Matters So Much

**Emotional Impact:** A character's voice, background music, and environmental sounds can set the mood in ways visuals cannot. The rumble of thunder can build tension. The soft hum of a refrigerator can create a sense of real life. Good audio helps the audience feel involved.

**Clarity of Dialogue:** If viewers cannot understand what characters are saying, they lose track of the story. Muffled or distorted dialogue ruins scenes. Clear sound keeps the audience focused on the plot.

**Professionalism:** Crisp, balanced audio signals that you took time to handle sound properly. Even if you have strong visuals, poor sound can make the project feel unfinished.

These reasons apply to all kinds of films, from low-budget shorts to large productions.

## 2. Basic Sound Equipment

Sound gear can be as simple or as complex as your budget allows. Let's look at the essential items:

1. **Microphones:**
   - **Shotgun Microphones**: Long, narrow mics designed to capture sound mainly from the front. They're often used on a boom pole above the actors to pick up dialogue clearly while reducing side noise.
   - **Lavalier (Lapel) Microphones**: Small mics clipped to a person's clothing. They're ideal for interviews or situations where a boom mic might be hard to use.
   - **Handheld Microphones**: Common for news or documentary work where the interviewer holds the mic near the person talking.
   - **Studio Condenser Microphones**: Used in voice-over or controlled indoor setups; they aren't usually brought to a film set, but they're important for ADR (Automated Dialogue Replacement) in post.
2. **Boom Pole:**
   - A long pole on which you can mount a shotgun mic. This lets you place the mic close to the actors without entering the frame. The closer the mic is to the sound source, the clearer the audio.
3. **Wind Protection (Blimps and Windshields):**
   - If you're shooting outdoors, wind noise can ruin recordings. A "dead cat" (the fuzzy cover) or a blimp (a hollow windshield enclosure) helps block wind. Even indoors, small drafts from air conditioners can cause unwanted noise.
4. **Audio Recorder or Mixer:**
   - Some cameras let you plug a mic directly into them, but many filmmakers use a separate audio recorder to capture higher-quality sound and have more control over levels.
   - A field mixer can help you adjust volume for multiple mics, monitor levels with headphones, and record onto memory cards.
5. **Headphones:**
   - You should always monitor your recordings with closed-back headphones that block outside noise. This helps you detect hums or buzzing before they spoil your track.
6. **Cables and Adapters:**
   - Audio connections can be XLR, mini-jack (3.5mm), or other formats. Make sure you have the right cables for your mics and recorder. Keep extras because cables can fail.

## 3. Single-System vs. Double-System Sound

1. **Single-System:**
   - The mic plugs directly into the camera, and the audio is recorded onto the same file as the video.
   - Easier to manage because you don't have to sync audio in post.
   - But camera preamps (the device that amplifies the microphone signal) are sometimes lower quality, leading to noisier recordings.
2. **Double-System:**
   - You record audio on a separate device. The camera captures video without the audio track, or with a scratch audio track (a low-quality guide track).
   - Higher audio quality, more channels, better mixing control.
   - You must sync audio with the video in post, often by using a clapperboard or a quick hand clap at the start of each take.

Professionals often prefer double-system because of the improved sound control. However, single-system can work on smaller shoots or for quick interviews if your camera's audio input is decent.

---

## 4. Techniques for Recording Dialogue

**Boom Technique:**

- A boom operator stands just outside the camera's frame, holding the mic overhead. The tip of the mic points toward the actor's mouth. This captures clear dialogue and minimal background noise.
- The operator must be alert and move with the actors, keeping the mic aimed correctly. They also watch for shadows the mic or pole might cast on set.

**Lavalier Placement:**

- When using a lav mic, clip it where it can pick up the actor's voice without rubbing against clothing. Hiding it under shirts can lead to rustling sounds.
- Some people use small covers or special tape to secure a lav in place. Test for clothing noise before recording.

**Mic Distance:**

- The closer the mic is to the actor, the cleaner the recording. You want to reduce the echo from the room. Be careful not to get the mic into the shot, though.
- If the mic is too far away, you pick up more ambient noise. If it's too close, you might get boomy or distorted sound.

**Multiple Actors:**

- In scenes with multiple people talking, you can use multiple lavs, or you can move the boom mic from person to person as they speak.
- A skilled boom operator can "cue" (quickly swing the mic) to the current speaker. This requires practice.

---

## 5. Handling Ambient Noise

Real environments have sounds like traffic, air conditioners, or people talking off-screen. Sometimes these noises add realism, but they can also drown out dialogue. Here are some ways to deal with ambient sound:

1. **Location Scouting:**
    - Before shooting, visit the location and listen. Is there a noisy road nearby? A barking dog? A refrigerator that hums? Plan how to handle these.
    - You might decide to unplug the fridge during takes (but remember to plug it back in later!). Or you might pick a time of day when traffic is lighter.
2. **Room Tone:**
    - Record 30 seconds to 1 minute of the location's "silence" with no talking. This captures the natural hum of the place.
    - Later, you can use room tone in editing to fill gaps or smooth out audio transitions. If you cut a line of dialogue, you can slip in a bit of room tone so the background stays consistent.
3. **Mic Choice:**
    - A highly directional shotgun mic can help reject side noise. A lav mic, placed carefully, might catch less echo in a big room.
4. **Sound Blankets and Acoustic Panels:**

- If you have control over the location, you can hang blankets or foam to reduce echoes or outside noise. Even simple thick drapes can help.
- For example, if you're in a large empty room, you can place blankets against the walls to reduce the echo.

---

## 6. Reducing Wind and Handling Outdoor Setups

**Wind Noise:**

- Outdoors, always use a windscreen or a "dead cat" over your shotgun mic. Even a slight breeze can create rumbling sounds.
- Point the mic away from strong gusts if possible. Shield it with your body or a portable wind blocker.

**Car Scenes:**

- Recording inside a moving car can be loud due to engine noise and road sounds. Sometimes you can place lav mics on the actors, then record with windows up.
- Another approach is to shoot the car scene in a controlled environment (like towing the car on a trailer) and record dialogue more clearly. If that's not possible, you might plan to redo the lines later in ADR.

**Crowded Public Spaces:**

- If you film in a busy street, the background might be too loud. You can get special permissions to film during quieter times or use directional mics and get close to your actors.
- In worst-case scenarios, you might record reference audio on set, then re-record the dialogue in a quieter setting and match it to the lip movements later.

---

## 7. Recording Sound Effects On Set

**Foley** is usually done in post-production, but you can also grab some unique sounds while you're on location. For instance, if your scene involves footsteps in gravel, you can do a separate recording of footsteps with a mic close to the ground. This extra material can be very handy in post, especially if the original track was muddy. Make a note or a label of each recording so you remember what it's for. Sometimes these on-set recordings (room tone, footsteps, object hits) are "gold," because they capture the natural reverb of the location.

## 8. Working with a Sound Recordist or Mixer

On a bigger production, you might have a dedicated sound recordist or sound mixer. They:

- Manage the audio recorder and levels.
- Monitor each mic feed with headphones.
- Communicate with the boom operator about mic placement.
- Label each take so it's easy to organize later.

This person is vital. Let them check everything before you start filming. If they hear a hum or a bad cable, it's better to fix it right away than to discover the problem after hours of shooting. Treat your sound team with respect—they are saving you from big headaches in editing.

## 9. Monitoring Levels and Avoiding Distortion

**Audio Levels:**

- When you record, you see a volume meter on the recorder or camera screen. This meter usually goes from around -60 dB (very soft) to 0 dB (where audio clips or distorts).
- Aim for peaks around -12 dB to -6 dB. That gives you some headroom in case someone suddenly speaks louder than expected.
- If the levels go above 0 dB, the sound becomes clipped (distorted), which is often impossible to fix in post.

**Headphone Monitoring:**

- Besides watching the meter, always listen with headphones. A meter might look fine, but you could have a faint hum or crackle. Headphones help you catch these issues right away.

## 10. Syncing Sound in Post-Production

If you use **double-system**, you have separate audio and video files. You must sync them:

1. **Clapperboard**: The most common method. You film the clapperboard snapping shut, and the audio track picks up the "clap" sound. In editing software, you align the visual of the clap with the audio spike.
2. **Manual Sync**: If you forgot a clapperboard, you can use a hand clap or look at a moment the actor's mouth is clearly open for a word and match it to the audio.
3. **Software**: Some editing programs have automatic syncing tools if the camera recorded a scratch track. They analyze waveforms to match them up.

Always label each recording with scene and take numbers so you can find the matching files easily. Good organization saves you from chaos later.

---

## 11. Wireless Systems

**Wireless Microphone Kits** let your actors move freely without cables:

- The actor wears a transmitter pack connected to the lav mic.
- The sound recordist has a receiver.
- You must check for interference and the battery level on both ends.
- Wireless signals can drop out if the actor is too far away or in a crowded frequency area.

In some places, certain frequencies are licensed for broadcast or emergency services, so you must pick an open frequency. Always do a range test before filming an important scene.

---

## 12. Dealing with Echo or "Roomy" Sound

Large rooms with hard surfaces reflect sound, causing echoes. Actors' lines sound hollow or distant. Possible fixes:

- Bring furniture or rugs to absorb reflections.

- Place portable acoustic panels behind the camera or along walls.
- If it's still too echoey, consider capturing enough reference audio to replace the dialogue later with ADR. But that's a lot of work, so many prefer to fix the room if possible.

## 13. Backing Up Your Audio

Just like you protect your video files, you must back up audio. If you're recording to memory cards, copy them to at least two hard drives. Keep a note of the track names or numbers for each day of shooting. Accidents happen, and losing sound files is painful. If your recorder can record two copies at once (dual recording feature), enable it to reduce risk.

## 14. Planning for ADR (Automated Dialogue Replacement)

Sometimes, no matter how much care you take, certain lines are unusable. Actors might have to re-record them in a sound studio:

- **ADR Process:** The actor watches the scene and attempts to match their own lip movements. A sound engineer records them in a quiet, controlled booth.
- **Matching Performance:** The actor tries to recreate the same emotion. This can be hard.
- **Ambient Matching:** You might add room tone or reverb to blend the new lines with the original environment.

ADR can save scenes, but it's time-consuming and can feel less natural. It's better to get clean audio on set whenever possible.

## 15. Practical Tips to Save Time and Stress

- **Call "Quiet on Set":** Ask everyone not involved in the scene to stay silent. Ambient chatter or phone alerts can spoil takes.
- **Wait for Planes or Traffic:** If an airplane roars overhead or a truck drives by, pause filming. It might only take 10 seconds to pass, but it saves hours in post.

- **Check Heaters/AC:** Turn off noisy units if they bleed into the recording.
- **Keep Records:** Have someone note which takes have good audio and which have problems.

## 16. Sound Mixer's Role in Real Time

A dedicated sound mixer will be adjusting levels live. They might boost the mic a bit if the actor speaks softly or lower it if the actor suddenly yells. This prevents clipping and keeps the dialogue well-balanced. They also might apply a high-pass filter to reduce low rumbles (like traffic or HVAC noise). Quick thinking by the mixer can make the difference between clean, usable audio and a messed-up track.

## 17. Capturing Surround Ambience

If your film has scenes where atmosphere is vital—like a busy marketplace or a forest—you can record a dedicated ambience track. Use stereo mics or a specialized surround recorder. This track can be layered under dialogue to make the location feel alive. Record a couple of minutes of just that ambience (with no talking) so you have a solid loop for editing.

## 18. The Boom Operator's Skills

Handling a boom pole all day is tough. Your arms can get tired, you must keep the mic out of the shot, and you have to follow actors who move unpredictably. Key pointers:

1. **Stamina and Positioning:** The boom operator often holds the pole above head height. Practice holding it for extended periods or rest it on your chest or a harness when possible.
2. **Mic Aim:** Keep the tip of the shotgun mic pointing at the speaker's mouth or chest area, about a foot or two above.
3. **Avoid Shadows:** Watch that you don't cast a shadow on the actor or set.
4. **Stay Quiet:** The slightest bump or movement on the pole can transfer noise to the mic. Move slowly and carefully.

## 19. Checking Playback

Sometimes you record a quick test or partial take and immediately listen back. If you notice a hiss or an odd echo, it's better to solve it before committing to the entire scene. Quick checks save major fixes later. If something is off, consider adjusting mic placement or moving a noisy object out of range.

## 20. Using a Slate App or Digital Tools

If you don't have a physical clapperboard, there are phone apps that mimic one. They display scene and take info and create a beep or clapping sound. This can help you sync if you're doing double-system. Make sure the beep is loud enough for the mic to pick up. Also, note that your phone's brightness might reflect in reflective surfaces, so watch your angles.

## 21. Shooting Scenes with Singing or Music

If your film has a musical number or an actor singing, you might:

- **Pre-Record the Track:** The actor lip-syncs on set. Then the final version is mixed in later.
- **Live Singing:** You record them actually singing. You need a controlled set and possibly multiple microphones to capture their voice and any instruments.
- **Playback System:** If the actor is dancing or singing in sync with a track, you need a small speaker to play the music. But watch for bleed into the dialogue mic. Often, you only keep a tiny reference from the on-set track and replace it in post.

## 22. Taking Advantage of Modern Technology

Many digital recorders today have helpful tools:

- **Dual Recording:** Records two tracks at different levels, so if the main track clips, the second track is still safe at a lower volume.

- **Built-In Limiters:** Helps keep sudden peaks under control.
- **Auto-Mix Features:** Some advanced mixers can lower unused mics automatically to reduce background noise when the person wearing that mic isn't talking.

Still, it's best not to rely solely on auto settings. A human ear and good technique outperform any gadget.

## 23. Troubleshooting Common Problems

- **Hum or Buzz:** Could be a grounding issue with cables or interference from nearby electronics. Try a different cable or move away from fluorescent lights or certain power lines.
- **Popping "P" Sounds (Plosives):** If you're very close to the mic, certain consonants cause a burst of air. Use a pop filter or angle the mic slightly off-axis.
- **Rustling Clothes:** Reposition the mic or ask the actor to wear different fabric if possible. Pin the clothing tighter so it doesn't flap.
- **Loose Connections:** Check that your XLR cables click in firmly. A half-inserted connection can cause static.

## 24. Listening for Consistency

If you're shooting a long scene over several days, try to match the same microphone placement. If on Day 1 the lav is on the actor's chest, and on Day 2 it's near the collar, the sound might differ. Keep notes or take reference pictures of how you placed the mic so you can replicate it.

## 25. Chapter 9 Key Points Recap

- Sound quality is as important as visuals. Poor audio can distract viewers from your story.
- Use decent microphones (shotgun, lav, or both) and learn correct placement.

- Decide between single-system (recording into the camera) or double-system (separate recorder).
- Control ambient noise by scouting quiet times, using room tone, and applying wind protection outdoors.
- Monitor levels closely. Avoid clipping. Listen with good headphones for hums or crackles.
- Use a clapperboard or other methods to sync audio in post if you record double-system.
- A dedicated sound recordist or mixer can save you from trouble.
- Back up your audio files to multiple drives. Keep them labeled and organized.

By following these guidelines, you can capture crisp, clear dialogue and ambient sounds for your film. Next, in Chapter 10, we'll look at **designing the look of your film**. This covers sets, locations, costumes, and props—everything that appears on camera. Sound and visuals together shape your movie's identity, so let's explore how to craft the perfect on-screen world.

# CHAPTER 10: DESIGNING THE LOOK OF YOUR FILM

When you watch a movie, you notice the sets, costumes, and props just as much as the characters. This overall appearance is often called **production design**. A well-designed film world can transport the audience to a different place or time, making the story more engaging. Even if you have a limited budget, you can still design interesting visuals by carefully picking and arranging what appears on camera. In this chapter, we'll explore how to develop a consistent look, find or build sets, choose costumes, and manage props. We'll also talk about color schemes and small details that bring your film's style to life.

## 1. The Role of Production Design

Production design involves everything from large-scale sets to tiny objects in the background. It sets the visual tone and helps tell the story without words. A messy desk full of old papers can show a character's untidy life. A sleek, modern apartment might hint that the character is wealthy or loves minimal style. By planning these elements, you help viewers understand the mood and the characters before a line is spoken.

## 2. Early Planning with a Production Designer

If your team is big enough, you might have a **production designer** who oversees sets, props, and costumes. On smaller projects, the director or producer often takes this job. Whichever the case, start planning early:

1. **Read the Script:** Note every location, item, or clothing piece that feels important. For example, if a character always wears a red scarf, that's a key detail.
2. **Brainstorm Style Ideas:** Will the film look gritty and realistic, or bright and playful? Are the locations modern or old-fashioned?
3. **Create Mood Boards or References:** Gather photos or drawings that capture the style you want. This could include paintings, historical photos, magazine clippings, or screenshots from other films.

This prep work helps guide all design decisions. It also helps communicate the vision to your team.

---

## 3. Choosing Locations vs. Building Sets

**Real Locations:**

- Often cheaper, because you don't have to build anything.
- They come with existing details—furniture, architectural style, etc.
- Less control over layout. If you need to move a wall for camera angles, that's not possible.
- Permits might be required, or owners might limit what you can do.

**Sets on a Stage:**

- Full control over design and layout. You can build walls, paint them, or remove them for wide camera shots.
- You can control lighting without worrying about windows.
- Costs more, since you have to build or rent the space, materials, and labor.
- Perfect for fantasy or historical settings that are hard to find in real life.

For smaller projects, real locations are common. You can dress them up with props and small changes. Even a friend's apartment can look like a cozy set if you rearrange the furniture and add decorations.

---

## 4. Dressing Locations

When you use a real location, you might need to rearrange or bring your own items to fit the script. This process is called **set dressing**:

1. **Remove Clutter:** If you're filming in someone's living room, remove personal photos or things that don't match your character's life.
2. **Add Story Elements:** If the character is a painter, place some brushes, a half-finished canvas, and paint tubes around. If they are a tech genius, include computer parts, wires, or schematics on the walls.
3. **Keep Continuity in Mind:** Mark where items are placed. If you move a lamp for a different shot, remember to put it back.

4. **Keep it Realistic:** Too many props can feel fake. The space should look lived-in but not overly staged.

A small budget can still achieve a strong design by focusing on key details. One unique painting or a distinctive piece of furniture can speak volumes about the character.

---

## 5. Costumes and Wardrobe

Clothes tell the audience about a character's personality, social status, and era. Think carefully about each character's wardrobe:

- **Color Palette:** Does your film have a certain color scheme? Maybe muted tones for a sad drama or bright pastels for a fun story. The costumes should fit into this palette.
- **Character Consistency:** A sloppy character might wear wrinkled shirts or mismatched socks. A polished businessperson might have perfectly pressed suits.
- **Period Accuracy:** If your film is set in the 1980s, avoid modern logos or styles. Do some research to make sure the clothes feel right for the time.
- **Multiple Outfits:** If your script covers many days, characters might change clothes. Keep track of which outfit belongs to which scene. Label them or store them carefully so you don't confuse them.

For a big production, a **costume designer** and team might sew custom pieces. For a smaller film, you can shop at thrift stores or ask actors to bring their own clothes that match the style. Just make sure everything stays consistent.

---

## 6. Props: Big and Small

Props are the items characters use or see on screen, such as phones, guns, books, or coffee cups. They can be important story devices (like a special key) or just set dressing (like magazines on a table). Tips for managing props:

1. **Prop List:** Read the script and list every object that appears in each scene. This helps you avoid forgetting anything.

2. **Accuracy:** If your scene is set in the 1950s, don't use a modern smartphone as a prop. If a character handles a tool, make sure it's something that fits the character's job.
3. **Hero Props:** Items that get close-ups or are crucial to the plot need to look good. Invest more time or money on them.
4. **Duplicates:** If a prop breaks or is part of a stunt, have spares. Nothing slows production like a broken prop you can't replace.

Props must be stored and labeled, especially if you have many. A dedicated props person or the production designer often keeps track of them between takes.

## 7. Color Theory and Visual Unity

Colors affect how viewers feel. Red can indicate danger or passion, while blue can be calm or cold. You can plan a color scheme that runs throughout the film. For example:

- **Monochromatic:** Various shades of one color, giving a focused look.
- **Complementary:** Opposite colors on the color wheel (like orange and blue) create strong contrast.
- **Analogous:** Neighboring colors (like red, orange, and yellow) for a softer transition.

Let's say your main character always wears something yellow, symbolizing hope. You might put splashes of yellow in the background to tie the scenes together. Or maybe the sets are mostly muted, and the character's bright outfit stands out. A consistent color strategy can unify your movie visually.

## 8. Research and References

If your film takes place in a specific time or culture, do in-depth research:

- **Historical Films:** Look up photos, paintings, or old catalogs to see how rooms and clothes looked.
- **Fantasy or Sci-Fi:** You might look at concept art or other movies for inspiration. Decide what sets your world apart.

- **Regional Setting:** If it's set in a real-world city, examine local architecture, sign styles, or typical building materials.

The more you know about the setting, the more authentic your design choices become. Even small details (like the style of doorknobs or the pattern on curtains) can add believability.

---

## 9. Making the Most of a Tight Budget

Not all films have the funds to build elaborate sets. Here are budget-friendly ideas:

1. **Borrow or Rent Items:** Ask friends or community groups for furniture, props, or decorations. Thrift stores can be goldmines for cheap pieces.
2. **Minimalist Approach:** If your story allows, keep the set simple. Use a few striking objects or color blocks. Let lighting and framing carry the style.
3. **Reuse and Redress:** The same location can serve different purposes with slight changes in decor or camera angles. Move furniture, change the lighting, swap out a few props, and you have a "new" spot.
4. **Crafty Solutions:** If you need a futuristic control panel, you could paint cardboard shapes and add some LED strips. It may look fine on camera if done neatly.

With creativity, you can design a convincing world without spending a fortune.

---

## 10. Collaboration with Other Departments

Your production design team should work closely with the director, cinematographer, and lighting crew:

- **Director:** Approves the overall style and checks if the design fits the story.
- **Cinematographer:** Lighting choices can affect how colors appear. A bright red set might look washed out under a certain light.
- **Costume Department:** You don't want the walls to be the same color as the main character's outfit unless that's intentional. Also, avoid clothes that reflect too much light or create moiré patterns on camera.

Good communication prevents surprises. You don't want to paint a room green only to discover the cinematographer planned to do green screen work there.

## 11. Set Construction Basics

If you do build sets:

1. **Scale and Materials:** Use lightweight materials like plywood or flats. Remember that the camera only sees what's in front of it, so you might not need a full 360-degree set.
2. **Paint:** A fresh coat of paint can totally change a location's mood. You can add texture by sponging or layering colors.
3. **Safety:** Make sure your set is stable. If you have raised platforms or fake walls, secure them so nobody gets hurt.
4. **Time and Labor:** Building even a small set takes time. Schedule enough days for painting, drying, and setup.

On some productions, the art department can build partial sets that match real locations, expanding them. For instance, you might build a small corner of a spaceship interior and then only show that corner from a few angles with the right lighting.

## 12. Continuity Across Scenes

If your story returns to a location multiple times, you need consistency. If a picture frame is crooked in Scene 2, it should still be crooked in Scene 4 unless there's a reason it moved. The same applies to costumes: if the character spilled coffee on their shirt, it needs to remain there unless the script says they changed clothes. Keep notes or photos of each scene setup. Mark the floor for furniture positions. This helps avoid accidental changes when you come back another day to shoot.

## 13. Background Extras and Dressing

If you have extras (background actors) in a busy scene, they're part of the visual design. Their clothes should fit the setting. A high school hallway scene might have students with backpacks, casual clothes, posters on the walls, and lockers. A medieval fantasy market might have extras wearing cloaks, carrying baskets, and some smoke in the background from a blacksmith stall. The background atmosphere can make or break the believability of your environment.

---

## 14. Small Details with Big Impact

Sometimes, a small item can define a character or a location:

- **Character's Signature Item:** A detective's old-fashioned pocket watch, a scholar's antique pen, or a musician's worn-down guitar. These objects can become iconic.
- **Wall Decorations:** Posters, paintings, or signs. They reveal the character's interests or the location's vibe.
- **Repeated Motifs:** Maybe a spiral design appears in the wallpaper, on the character's necklace, and in the company logo. This can tie the film's visuals together in a subtle way.

These details show that you put thought into every corner of the frame, making the world feel real and rich.

---

## 15. Working with Special Effects and Green Screens

If you plan to composite backgrounds later, you still need some design elements for the actors to interact with:

- **Partial Set Pieces:** For example, if a character stands on a cliff that will be CG in the final shot, build a small platform with real rocks to match the CG environment's look.
- **Prop Interaction:** If there's a CG creature, maybe the actor holds a practical harness or dummy so their hands match the creature's body in the final.
- **Matching Color and Lighting:** If the final background is a dark, stormy sky, don't dress your set in bright warm tones. The mismatch will be obvious.

Plan carefully so everything lines up. Talk with the visual effects team about what they need from you.

## 16. Scheduling for Design Work

Production design tasks can take longer than you expect:

- **Scouting and Dressing Locations:** You might need a day or two before shooting to rearrange furniture and hang decorations.
- **Building Sets:** This can take weeks if it's large or detailed.
- **Collecting Costumes and Props:** Shopping, renting, or creating items can be time-consuming.
- **Striking the Set:** After filming, you often need to return locations to their original condition.

Build these steps into your schedule. Don't wait until the last minute or the set might look rushed.

## 17. Testing on Camera

Sometimes a costume color or set paint looks different on camera than it does to the eye. Film a test if you can:

- **Check under actual lighting:** If the cinematographer is using bright, warm lights, that pale green wall might look like lime.
- **Move the actor around:** Make sure the costume works from different angles. Flimsy materials might show wrinkles or glare.
- **Look for Moiré or Flicker:** Certain patterns can cause strange effects on digital cameras. Avoid tight stripes or weird textures that cause flicker.

Doing a quick camera test can prevent unwanted surprises during the real shoot.

## 18. Organizing and Storing Items

If you have many costumes or props, store them in a labeled system. For example:

- **Costume Racks** with name tags for each character.

- **Prop Boxes** labeled by scene ("Scene 5 – Kitchen Items").
- **Design Binders** or digital folders with reference photos, receipts, or rental agreements.

When it's time to film a scene, you can quickly grab the correct outfit or prop without wasting time searching.

---

## 19. Reusing and Recycling

A smart way to handle design on a tight budget is to reuse items:

- Paint the same flats differently for a new set.
- Use the same clothing in different scenes with small changes (add a jacket, change accessories).
- Turn a living room set into a bedroom by swapping furniture and adjusting decoration.

Your creativity in repurposing items can stretch your budget while maintaining variety on screen.

---

## 20. Working with Real Objects vs. Replicas

If your character uses a firearm, you might use:

- **Real (Disabled) Gun or a Blank-Firing Gun:** Needs safety checks and often an expert on set.
- **Replica or Prop Gun:** Safer, but can look very realistic on camera. You can add muzzle flashes in post.

For food scenes, sometimes you use real food, but keep in mind it spoils quickly under hot lights. You can also use fake or plastic food for background shots. For breakable items like glass, you might use **sugar glass** or **breakaway props** designed to shatter more safely.

## 21. Keeping the Look Consistent

Your film might have many locations and times of day. Yet, you want a unifying style. Maybe that style is warm, with brown and orange tones in every location. Or maybe it's a slightly futuristic angle with clean lines and minimal decoration. Keep these concepts in mind for every design decision, whether it's a small alley scene or a big indoor set. If you switch styles without reason, the audience may feel confused.

---

## 22. Handling Damaged or Aged Items

If your story requires a worn-down environment, you can do some **aging**:

- **Distress Costumes:** Use sandpaper or a cheese grater to make clothes look worn. Add stains or tears.
- **Weather Props:** Paint cracks or rust. Add dust or scuff marks.
- **Break Windows or Walls:** Use safe breakaway materials, or carefully create cracks.
- **Burned Edges of Paper:** Be very careful with fire. Do it outside or with a fire extinguisher nearby.

These small touches help sell the idea that the location or items have a history.

---

## 23. Checking Cultural and Legal Issues

Be aware of:

- **Copyrighted Brands:** Showing real brand logos in your film can cause legal concerns unless you have permission. You might hide or cover them, or create a fake brand logo.
- **Offensive Imagery:** Decorations or symbols can have meanings you didn't realize. Research thoroughly to avoid offending viewers.
- **Historical Accuracy:** If you claim a certain period, don't mix in anachronistic items. Some history buffs will notice.

This step ensures you won't run into trouble after your film is released.

## 24. Final Touches on the Day

Right before you start shooting, walk through the set:

- **Check Props:** Are they in the correct place? Are they clean or dusty as intended?
- **Inspect Costumes:** No wrinkles or unexpected stains? Are they the right outfit for the scene number?
- **Hide Modern Clutter:** If your film is set in 1920, remove cell phones, cables, or modern signs that could appear in the background.
- **Lighting Harmony:** If the cinematographer has changed the lighting from your test, do you need to shift the color of any items?

A quick run-through can catch small mistakes that would stand out on camera.

---

## 25. Chapter 10 Key Points Recap

- Production design shapes the film's visual world: sets, props, and costumes.
- Start with the script, note important items, and decide on an overall style or color palette.
- Pick between real locations and built sets. Dress locations with relevant items to fit the story.
- Costumes should reflect character personality and fit the time period. Keep them organized for continuity.
- Manage props with care. Prepare duplicates for breakable or important items.
- Use color theory to create a consistent look. Research historical or cultural details for authenticity.
- Plan enough time and labor for building, painting, or decorating sets.
- Test your designs on camera to ensure colors and textures look correct.
- Stay organized, label your items, and maintain continuity across scenes.

With your film's on-set audio covered and a well-designed visual world, you're well on your way to a professional production. In the next chapters, we'll see how all these elements come together when you step on set as a director, guide your actors, and manage a smooth shoot. By coordinating design, sound, and performance, you'll bring your script to life in front of the camera.

# CHAPTER 11: LEADING THE PRODUCTION AS A DIRECTOR

You have a script, a team, and a plan for how your film should look and sound. Now it's time to focus on directing. The director is the person who shapes how each scene is filmed, how the actors perform, and how the movie feels overall. This chapter explains the director's responsibilities, how to make choices under pressure, and ways to communicate so that everyone on set works well together. We'll talk about practical tips that help you keep control of the production while still allowing room for creative ideas. By the end, you'll know what tasks a director must handle each day and how to keep your set running smoothly.

## 1. The Director's Main Role

A director is often seen as the "leader" of the film set. But what does that mean?

1. **Interpreting the Script:** You turn the written words into images and sounds. That includes deciding on shot choices, pacing, mood, and style.
2. **Guiding Actors:** You make sure each actor knows who their character is, how they feel in each scene, and why they do what they do.
3. **Coordinating with Crew:** You talk with the cinematographer, production designer, sound team, and more. You make sure everyone's work matches the film's vision.
4. **Problem-Solving:** If something breaks or an actor can't show up, you decide how to adjust the plan without losing the story's impact.

The director must also balance creativity with the practical side of filmmaking. Your day isn't just about cool ideas. It's about making the best use of limited time and resources.

## 2. Pre-Production Tasks

Most of the director's important work happens before the camera rolls. Pre-production is where you make plans so your shoot goes well.

1. **Breaking Down the Script:** Go through each scene. Figure out the key actions, emotional beats, and story points. Plan which scenes are crucial and which can be simpler.
2. **Shot Lists and Storyboards:** You can list out which angles or movements you want for each scene. Storyboards are drawings that show how each frame might look. These help you and your cinematographer plan the lighting and camera setups.
3. **Location Visits:** By walking around each planned location, you can see where to place the camera, how the light looks at different times of day, and if there are any noise problems.
4. **Casting Input:** You work with the casting director or producer to choose actors who fit each role. Sometimes you hold auditions or watch audition tapes. You might also talk with actors about their ideas for the character.
5. **Rehearsals:** If possible, you meet with the actors before filming. You run through scenes so everyone has a sense of timing and motivation. This also helps you spot any weak spots in the script.

---

## 3. Communication on Set

A film set can be busy, with lights being moved, cables on the floor, and many people asking questions. As the director, you must communicate clearly and respectfully:

1. **Using a Calm Tone:** If you shout or panic, the crew may get tense. Speak firmly but calmly, even when you're under pressure.
2. **Talking to Department Heads:** Usually, you speak to the cinematographer (for visuals), the production designer (for set look), the sound mixer (for audio), and so on. Each of these heads handles the details in their department. You don't have to give instructions to every crew member yourself.
3. **Listening to Ideas:** Crew members have expertise. If your cinematographer suggests a slight change in camera angle for a better shot, consider it. If an actor has an idea for a line, hear them out. You can decide if it fits or not, but listening builds trust.
4. **Being Decisive:** While it's good to be open, you can't spend all day debating. When time is tight, you must pick a path and move on. A clear decision keeps the production rolling.

## 4. Working with the Assistant Director (AD)

On larger sets, there's usually a First Assistant Director (1st AD). They help with scheduling, keeping track of time, and making sure the production stays on target:

1. **Time Management:** The AD announces how long each setup should take, when meals happen, and when actors should be ready.
2. **Coordinating Crew:** The AD can call out "Quiet on set!" or line everyone up for the next shot. They handle logistics so you can focus on creative decisions.
3. **Safety and Rules:** They also watch for safety hazards or if anyone is not following rules on set.

If you're on a small production, you might not have an AD. In that case, you or the producer might handle these tasks. But whenever possible, having an AD frees the director to focus on directing.

---

## 5. Running a Typical Day on Set

When filming starts, a normal day has a sequence:

1. **Call Time:** Everyone arrives at a set time. The crew starts setting up lights and gear. Actors go to hair, make-up, or wardrobe.
2. **Rehearsal:** You walk through the scene with the actors. The cinematographer sees the action so they can plan camera moves. The sound team checks mic placement.
3. **Blocking:** You decide exactly where actors stand or move. You mark positions on the floor if needed.
4. **Lighting Setup:** The cinematographer and lighting crew place lights according to the plan. This can take time. You might talk with actors or prepare for the next scene during this.
5. **Camera Rehearsal:** You do a run-through with the camera rolling or not rolling, so the operator can practice moves.
6. **Shoot the Scene:** You call "Action!" The scene is performed. You watch carefully for any mistakes in performance or technical issues.
7. **Review and Adjust:** If the take is good but you want a different angle or if there was a sound problem, you do another take.

8. **Move to Next Setup:** Once you're satisfied, you move on to the next shot or scene. The crew repositions lights and gear.

You repeat this until all planned shots are done for the day. At the end, you might review some footage or talk with the AD about the next day's plan.

---

## 6. Handling Pressure and Time Limits

Time is often the biggest enemy on set. You might have only a few hours of sunlight, or a location might only be available for one day. Learn to handle pressure:

1. **Prioritize Key Shots:** If you're behind schedule, focus on the shots that are absolutely needed to tell the story. You can drop or shorten less important shots.
2. **Stay Flexible:** If the light isn't good for a planned shot, see if you can switch to another angle or scene.
3. **Keep People Motivated:** Stress can make people tired or short-tempered. Be polite and show respect. A positive tone can keep the team working at their best.
4. **Know When to Move On:** If you keep trying to get a perfect take, you might lose the chance to film other scenes. Accept a good-enough take if time is almost up.

---

## 7. Motivating the Crew

Filmmaking involves standing around, heavy lifting, and repeating tasks. A tired crew might lose energy or focus. Here are tips to keep morale high:

1. **Acknowledgment:** Say "Thank you" when people solve problems or do good work.
2. **Breaks and Meals:** Follow the schedule for breaks. Give everyone a chance to rest and eat.
3. **Positive Atmosphere:** Even if problems arise, keep your tone constructive. Avoid blaming.
4. **Listening:** If someone spots a potential improvement, let them share it. They may have a trick that saves time or improves the shot.

A happy crew often works harder and is more creative.

## 8. Working with Actors During Filming

Actors look to the director for guidance. You set the emotional tone of each scene and help them deliver strong performances. Here are some quick points (though Chapter 12 will explore working with actors in more depth):

1. **Clear Direction:** Instead of saying "Be more intense," you might say, "Imagine you just saw your best friend in danger. Let that worry show in your eyes." This helps the actor act with a clear goal.
2. **Stay Focused on Character Goals:** The actor should always know what their character wants in the scene. Are they trying to get information, express love, or hide fear?
3. **Avoid Micro-Managing:** Give actors room to explore. You can adjust them with notes after a take, rather than controlling every small detail.
4. **Watch for Continuity:** If an actor changes how they stand or hold a prop between takes, it might cause problems in editing. A script supervisor can help track these details.

## 9. Checking the Monitor

These days, directors often watch the action on a monitor linked to the camera. This helps see framing, focus, and performance details. But be careful not to get stuck behind the monitor all day:

1. **Balance:** Sometimes you need to be near the actors to give them direction. Standing next to them can create a better connection than shouting from behind a monitor.
2. **Trust the Cinematographer:** They watch for exposure, camera moves, and other technical aspects. If you trust them, you can look at the actors more.
3. **Playback:** After a take, you might do a quick review. But constant replays slow the schedule. Decide when it's vital and when to trust your gut.

## 10. Dealing with Problems

On any set, problems happen. Gear breaks. An actor forgets lines. You lose time. A director must keep the movie on track:

1. **Stay Calm:** If you panic, everyone else will too. Show confidence, even if you feel stressed.
2. **Ask for Solutions:** Your crew might have quick fixes. A broken mic might be replaced with a lav mic. A location can't be used? Maybe you shoot a close-up against a neutral wall and fill in the background later.
3. **Keep Moving:** If one scene can't be done now, switch to another scene or a simpler shot. Don't waste time if you can help it.
4. **Protect the Story:** Always ask, "What does the audience really need to see or hear here?" If a detail is not crucial, you can adapt or cut it.

---

## 11. Working with the Producer or Studio

On some shoots, there's a producer or a studio representative who oversees money or has creative notes. As the director:

1. **Respect the Budget:** If the producer says you must cut costs, look for ways to simplify. Maybe you reduce the number of extras or remove a complex stunt.
2. **Explain Creative Choices:** If they question why you want a certain shot, calmly show how it serves the story. Many producers are open to good reasoning.
3. **Negotiate When Needed:** If a note goes against your vision but is not a deal-breaker, see if you can make it work. If you strongly disagree, present alternatives that still meet the producer's concerns.

---

## 12. Overseeing the "Look" and Tone

You worked with the production designer, cinematographer, and other departments to plan the style. On set, you ensure everything matches that plan:

1. **Costume Checks:** Does the outfit match the scene's mood and the actor's storyline?

2. **Set Dressing:** Are the props in the right place? Any item that looks out of place?
3. **Color Consistency:** If your color scheme is warm, make sure lighting or costume changes don't break that look unless it's intentional.
4. **Pacing and Energy:** If you want a fast, punchy scene, direct actors to speak faster or the camera to move more. If it's a slow, thoughtful scene, let them pause and breathe.

---

## 13. Avoiding Burnout

Directing can be exhausting. You must answer questions nonstop, solve issues, and keep the creative vision intact:

1. **Delegate:** Let department heads handle details in their areas. Trust them to do their jobs.
2. **Take Short Breaks:** Even a couple of minutes to drink water and clear your head can help you stay sharp.
3. **Plan Downtime:** If it's a long shoot, have a rest day in the schedule.
4. **Use a Notebook or Assistant:** Write down quick notes or have someone help track tasks. You can't remember everything.

---

## 14. Team Spirit and Shared Ownership

A film set works best when people feel they're part of something good, not just following orders:

1. **Give Credit:** Say things like, "That's a nice lighting idea. Thanks for bringing that up." This shows you value crew input.
2. **Share the Vision:** Remind the team of the story's purpose. If they know what emotional tone you aim for, they can offer better solutions.
3. **Stay Approachable:** Let people know they can bring concerns to you (or to the AD). Problems fester if people are scared to speak up.
4. **Keep a Positive Tone:** Even if things go wrong, approach it as, "How can we fix this?" instead of blaming.

## 15. Reviewing Footage as You Go

Some directors wait until the end of the day to watch dailies (the footage shot that day). Others only do quick checks after each major scene:

1. **Catch Mistakes Early:** If a focus was off or a performance was off, you can reshoot while the set is still prepared.
2. **Keep the Flow:** If you spend too long reviewing, you lose precious shooting time.
3. **Plan Tomorrow:** At day's end, you might watch key clips with your cinematographer or AD. You see if you missed anything vital.

---

## 16. Balancing Ego and Vision

You're in charge, but filmmaking is collaborative. Some directors get too attached to every idea. Others let themselves be pushed around:

1. **Stand by Important Choices:** If a shot or performance is key to the story, fight to keep it.
2. **Know When to Bend:** If a small detail is causing big delays or conflict, maybe compromise is better than holding up the entire day.
3. **Stay Open to Surprises:** Sometimes an actor's ad-lib line or a crew member's suggestion might improve the scene.

---

## 17. Handling Technology on Set

Your set might have monitors, data wrangling for memory cards, or special effects gear:

1. **Stay Up to Date:** Know the basics of digital filming, data backups, or any special rigs your production uses.
2. **Rely on Experts:** If you have a VFX supervisor or a digital imaging technician (DIT), ask for their input on any technical issues. They can help you avoid problems later.
3. **Planning Shots for Post:** If you have effects, remember you need clean plates (shots of the background without actors) or reference markers. The director ensures these are captured before striking the set.

## 18. Consistency with Performances

If your film is shot out of order (which is common), you must track how characters are feeling in each scene:

1. **Emotional Continuity:** If Scene 20 is shot before Scene 19, the actor must know how they felt at the end of Scene 18 or 19 to keep the flow.
2. **Physical Details:** If the character was injured in a previous scene, make sure the actor shows the same injury or limp.
3. **Scripts and Notes:** You might have a binder with notes on each scene's emotional state. The script supervisor can help track line changes and continuity.

## 19. Wrapping Each Day

At the end of the day:

1. **Check Next Day's Schedule:** Confirm call times, locations, and which scenes you'll film.
2. **Give Crew Updates:** If anything changed, let the AD or production manager inform everyone.
3. **Review Dailies:** Sometimes you watch the day's footage with key crew. You see if you need pickups (extra shots).
4. **Secure Gear and Sets:** Make sure everything is stored safely. If you're returning to the same set, note where props and furniture are.

## 20. Working Toward a Smooth Post-Production

The director has a big hand in post-production too, but your choices on set affect editing:

1. **Get Enough Coverage:** Film enough angles and close-ups so the editor can build a smooth sequence.
2. **Sound Quality:** If you push for clear audio on set, you save headaches later.

3. **Keep an Eye on Continuity:** The more consistent each take is, the easier the edit.
4. **Take Notes for the Editor:** If you have a special idea for a cut or transition, note it. The editor will appreciate the guidance.

---

## 21. Balancing Creativity and Practical Limits

You might have a grand vision for a scene with huge crowd shots, but only 5 extras showed up. Or you wanted a sunrise shot, but the sky is cloudy. A director must adapt:

1. **Use Clever Angles:** If you have fewer extras, shoot close-ups or partial frames so it looks more crowded.
2. **Change the Script if Needed:** If the weather isn't right, can you move the scene indoors or change it to a nighttime scene?
3. **Focus on What Matters:** The story is key. Find ways to keep the emotional impact, even if you can't get everything you imagined.

---

## 22. Staying True to the Story

When the schedule is tight, the director might feel forced to rush or skip scenes. Always ask: "Which scenes are crucial to the story's heart?" Don't cut those. If you must drop something, choose a scene that doesn't damage the main storyline. Or find a shorter way to cover the same point. Keeping the story clear is your top job.

---

## 23. Setting the Tone for the Whole Production

People look to the director's attitude. If you're organized and friendly, the set tends to run better:

1. **Professional Conduct:** Show up on time. Be prepared.
2. **Respect People's Roles:** Each crew member is trying to do their best. Don't talk down to them.
3. **Confidence with Openness:** Let others know you have a plan but are open to improvements.

When they see you handle stress in a calm way, they'll be calmer too.

## 24. Mentoring New Crew or Interns

Many sets have interns or inexperienced team members. As a director:

1. **Offer Quick Insights:** If you have time, explain why you chose a certain shot or blocking.
2. **Encourage Learning:** Let them watch or ask questions when you're not in the middle of a crucial moment.
3. **Remember They're Watching You:** Your behavior sets an example. If you remain respectful, they learn good habits.

## 25. Chapter 11 Key Points Recap

- The director shapes the story on set, guiding the visuals, actors, and overall feel.
- Pre-production is where you plan shots, rehearse actors, and align the team on the film's style.
- Good communication keeps everyone on track. Stay calm, be decisive, and respect each department's input.
- Time is tight on set, so prioritize key shots. Accept good takes rather than chasing perfection if you risk losing time for other scenes.
- Keep morale high. Show gratitude, give breaks, and stay positive.
- Keep an eye on story continuity, from emotional beats to physical details.
- Be flexible, solve problems quickly, and adapt if conditions change.
- Finish each day by reviewing what you got and preparing for the next.
- Maintain a respectful, professional atmosphere so the crew can do their best work.

With these principles, you'll be ready to handle the daily tasks of directing. Next, in Chapter 12, we look deeper at **guiding the actors**. We'll talk about building trust with them, helping them find their characters, and shaping performances that grab the audience. Acting is at the heart of most films, so let's learn how to bring out each actor's best work.

# CHAPTER 12: GUIDING THE ACTORS

Actors are the face of your story. No matter how good your script or visuals are, weak or unconvincing performances can lower the entire film's quality. In this chapter, we'll explore how to help actors become their characters, bring true emotion to each scene, and make sure the audience connects with them. From casting to on-set direction, we'll look at clear methods to shape performances without micromanaging every detail. By the end, you'll know how to talk with your cast in a way that sparks creativity and brings your story to life.

## 1. Importance of Good Performances

**Audience Connection:** Viewers often relate to characters more than anything else. If actors seem genuine, people forget they're watching a movie. They care about what happens.
**Story Depth:** A talented cast can add layers to the script. A simple line can become powerful if performed with true feeling.
**Credibility:** Even in a fantasy or sci-fi setting, believable actors make the world feel real. Bad acting reminds the audience it's just a film.

## 2. Casting Wisely

Casting is more than just picking someone who looks the part:

1. **Character Fit:** Does the actor capture the character's essence, personality, or energy?
2. **Chemistry with Others:** If two actors play close friends or lovers, do they click in auditions? If they're supposed to be enemies, can they portray tension?
3. **Range and Versatility:** Some roles need a broad emotional range. Check if the actor can handle both quiet, subtle moments and big emotional scenes.
4. **Commitment to the Project:** If your shoot runs several weeks, does the actor have the schedule free? Are they interested in the role enough to prepare?

A well-structured audition process helps you see if they're suitable. You might provide scenes (sides) for them to read or ask them to do improv to see how they handle surprises.

## 3. Building Trust Early

Actors often feel vulnerable because they are putting their emotions on display. A good relationship with the director lets them feel safe:

1. **Introduce Yourself:** Before shooting starts, spend some time with them to talk about the film's style, your approach, and any questions they have.
2. **Listen to Their Ideas:** They might have thoughts on the character's backstory, motivations, or mannerisms. Let them share. You can refine these ideas to fit the story.
3. **Use Positive Language:** Instead of "That was bad," say, "Let's try it another way. I think your character might be more hesitant here." This approach is helpful.
4. **Set Up Rehearsals:** Even short get-togethers to read lines or discuss scenes can build understanding. Actors know what you expect, and you see how they respond.

## 4. Character Discussions

Many actors build characters by asking questions. You can guide them:

1. **Backstory:** Even if it's not in the script, discuss where the character grew up, what their family was like, or important life events.
2. **Goals and Fears:** Every character wants something, even if it's small. They also might fear failure or pain. This drives how they behave.
3. **Relationships:** If two characters are siblings, they might have shared memories or rivalries. If they're boss and employee, there's a hierarchy.
4. **Changes Over Time:** How does the character evolve throughout the film? Does a shy person gain confidence? Does a happy character become bitter?

Giving actors this info (or working with them to create it) helps them act with purpose in each scene.

## 5. Directing Styles

Every director has their own style. Here are some common methods:

1. **Action-Based Direction:** You give actors a clear verb or action. For example, "Persuade him to stay," or "Hide your excitement." This helps the actor focus on doing something, not just showing an emotion.
2. **Emotional Cues:** You talk about what the character is feeling. "Your character is afraid of being caught, but also hopeful for a second chance."
3. **Improvisation:** In some scenes, you might let actors improv lines to find natural reactions. This can lead to surprising, genuine moments.
4. **Line Readings (Used Sparingly):** Telling an actor exactly how to say a line can help if they're stuck, but doing it too often can make them feel like a puppet.

You might blend these methods. The key is giving directions that spur creativity rather than block it.

## 6. Respecting Different Acting Techniques

Actors train in various methods, such as "Method Acting," "Meisner," or "Classical." Some focus on personal memories to spark emotion, while others rely on imagination and technique. As a director:

1. **Ask About Their Process:** If an actor uses personal memories, you might not need to push them with emotional triggers. If they prefer external methods, you might focus on physical actions or changes in voice.
2. **Avoid Forcing One Style:** Let them use the method that works best for them, as long as the performance suits the film.
3. **Offer Clear Goals, Not Just Emotions:** Telling an actor "be sadder" can be vague. Instead, say, "You see the photo of your child and realize you may never see them again." Let them find sadness through the situation.

## 7. Adjusting Performances

During filming, you might want a slight change in how an actor delivers a line. Here's how to do it effectively:

1. **Praise First:** "I like how you showed how angry you are at the start."
2. **Give a Specific Change:** "But this time, can you let that anger simmer and then come out more quietly toward the end?"
3. **Focus on the Reason:** If they understand why the character would do it differently, it feels natural.
4. **Watch for Overcorrection:** If they push too far the other way, gently guide them back.

It's like a dance: you lead them a bit, they respond, and you refine together until it fits the scene.

---

## 8. Helping Shy or Insecure Actors

Some actors are new or feel uneasy in front of the camera:

1. **Private Rehearsals:** If they're nervous around the whole crew, do a short practice off to the side.
2. **Small Steps:** Don't overwhelm them with too many notes at once. Tackle one issue at a time.
3. **Encourage Them:** Let them know what they're doing right. Confidence can boost their performance.
4. **Use Close-Ups Later:** Let them get comfortable with wide or medium shots first. They might feel more pressure with a camera right in their face.

---

## 9. Handling Strong Personalities

Some actors have big egos or strong opinions. This can cause tension if not managed:

1. **Stay Respectful:** Even if they're difficult, yelling or insulting them won't help. Remain calm and firm.

2. **Listen, Then Decide:** Hear their viewpoint. If it doesn't clash with the story, maybe you can adapt. If not, explain clearly why you must do it a certain way.
3. **Use Diplomacy:** If an actor wants the spotlight in every scene, remind them the script has other characters. Find a compromise if it doesn't hurt the story.
4. **Involve the Producer or AD If Needed:** If problems escalate, let higher-level staff mediate. You need the production to keep going.

## 10. Group Scenes and Ensemble Cast

When many actors share a scene, directing becomes more complex:

1. **Blocking for All:** Each actor needs a place to stand or move that feels natural and is visible to the camera.
2. **Focus of Attention:** If the scene is about one character's confession, guide others to react but not distract.
3. **Overlap or Silence?:** Decide if you want actors to talk over each other for realism or wait for lines. Overlapping can be authentic but can cause audio challenges.
4. **Rehearse the Flow:** A big scene with five or six talking characters might need multiple run-throughs to get the timing right.

## 11. Emotional Scenes and Intimate Moments

Scenes with crying, anger, or intimacy need extra care:

1. **Set the Right Environment:** Fewer crew around if it's a sensitive moment. Dim lights or quiet the set if it helps the actor concentrate.
2. **Discuss Boundaries for Intimate Scenes:** If there's hugging or kissing, talk with the actors about comfort levels. Some productions hire an intimacy coordinator to ensure everyone feels safe.
3. **Give Actors Space Before and After:** If an actor must cry on cue, let them prepare privately. After the scene, give them a moment to settle.
4. **No Pushing Past Safety:** Emotional or physical safety is key. Don't force an actor to do something they're uncomfortable with. Find a creative alternative.

## 12. When Actors Go Off-Script

Sometimes actors ad-lib lines or change the script:

1. **Check If It Improves the Scene:** If the new line feels natural and you like it, keep it. But confirm it doesn't clash with future lines or the story's logic.
2. **Get a "Scripted" Take Too:** If you have time, film the original lines as well. That way, the editor can choose later.
3. **Stay Consistent:** If the actor changes a major plot detail, you might need to adjust other scenes or dialogue. Weigh that carefully.
4. **Balance Freedom and Control:** Some directors love improv. Others want a tight script. Communicate your preference beforehand.

---

## 13. Handling Scenes with Stunts or Effects

If an actor must do a stunt or work with a special effect:

1. **Safety Briefing:** Work with the stunt coordinator to explain what will happen. The actor should understand any risk and how to minimize it.
2. **Acting Through Stunts:** Even if they're jumping away from an explosion, they still need to show fear, shock, or determination. Remind them of the character's mindset.
3. **Timing with Effects:** If there's a practical effect (like a fake wall breaking), the actor must react at the right moment. Rehearse carefully.
4. **Use Doubles if Needed:** If it's too dangerous or physically tricky, a stunt double can step in. Then the actor focuses on face expressions in close-ups.

---

## 14. Younger or Less Experienced Actors

When working with children or people who are new to acting:

1. **Simple Directions:** Avoid complicated emotional terms. Use easy language like "Be excited here, like you found a secret," or "You're scared someone might see you."

2. **Short Takes:** Kids might lose focus quickly. Plan shorter scenes or let them rest often.
3. **Games and Positivity:** Turn rehearsals into a game if it helps them loosen up. Praise good attempts.
4. **Guardian or Manager:** Children usually come with a parent or guardian. Keep them informed and comfortable with the process.

---

## 15. Voice and Dialogue Delivery

Some actors have strong voices but might rush lines. Others speak too softly:

1. **Pace:** If they talk too fast, remind them to slow down so the audience can follow. If too slow, encourage a quicker pace for energy.
2. **Diction:** If words are unclear, do exercises or ask them to speak with more clarity. But be mindful if the character's accent or style is supposed to be a bit mumbled.
3. **Volume and Projection:** Even with good microphones, an actor who mumbles can cause problems. Keep them aware of how loud they should speak.
4. **Pauses and Beats:** Some lines need a short pause for impact. Others should flow quickly. Help the actor find these rhythms.

---

## 16. Tracking Consistency Over Multiple Takes

When you do many takes, the actor might change small details:

1. **Props and Movement:** If they pick up the cup on "I can't believe it!" in one take, they should do the same in the next for continuity, unless you decide differently.
2. **Emotional Build:** The actor should maintain the same level of emotion for each line across different angles. A script supervisor or continuity person can help.
3. **Working with the Editor in Mind:** If the actor changes their accent or volume between takes, it's harder to cut them together. Keep track of these shifts.

## 17. Dealing with Line Flubs

Actors forget or mix lines. That's normal:

1. **Don't Scold:** It adds tension. Encourage them to try again.
2. **Try Prompting:** If it's just one tricky word, a quick reminder can help.
3. **Rewrite If Needed:** If a line is too hard or unnatural, consider a simpler wording that conveys the same meaning.
4. **Use a Cue Card Carefully:** Some sets place a hidden card with lines. But this can be risky if the actor's eyes keep darting to it.

---

## 18. Encouraging Natural Reactions

Sometimes the script calls for a real reaction, like surprise:

1. **Controlled Surprises:** You can coordinate a small surprise on set, like an unexpected sound, if the actor agrees. This can capture genuine shock.
2. **Improv Practice:** Let them respond to new lines from a scene partner. This keeps them alert.
3. **Focus on Listening:** Tell actors to truly listen to each other, not just wait for their turn to speak. Natural reactions come from hearing the other person's words as if new.

---

## 19. Knowing When You Got the Scene

Directors often struggle to decide if a take is "good enough":

1. **Check Key Points:** Did the actor hit the emotional note? Did the lines come across clearly? Does it match the story's overall tone?
2. **Watch for Authenticity:** Did the moment feel real, or forced? If it feels real, it likely is.
3. **Consider Coverage:** If you have a solid wide shot and a good close-up, you might not need dozens more angles.
4. **Time vs. Perfection:** If you keep chasing a "perfect" take, you risk losing time for other scenes. Set a limit or trust your instincts.

## 20. Coaching Actors in Post-Production

Sometimes you need to fix or enhance performances later:

1. **ADR for Lines:** If an actor's line was unclear or had noise, they can re-record it in a studio. They must match the original performance.
2. **Pickup Shots:** You might schedule a short extra shoot day for close-ups or reaction shots. This can help fill any gaps.
3. **Performance Tweaks Through Editing:** You can choose the best takes, reorder lines slightly, or cut around small mistakes. But editing can't fix everything if the core performance is weak.

---

## 21. Helping Actors with Stress

Shooting can be long and tiring. Actors might be worn out:

1. **Breaks:** If possible, allow them a moment to rest or get water.
2. **Patience:** If someone is flustered, a short breather can help them reset.
3. **Keep the Set Calm:** Avoid chaos or loud arguments near where actors prepare.
4. **Check In:** A quick "How are you feeling? Any concerns?" can build trust.

---

## 22. Collaborating with Choreographers, Coaches, or Trainers

Some films have special needs: dance sequences, fight scenes, or specific accents:

1. **Dance or Movement Coaches:** They help actors learn steps or physical actions. You coordinate how these actions fit the camera angles.
2. **Dialect Coaches:** If the actor must speak with a certain accent, a coach can drill them on pronunciation.
3. **Fight Choreographers:** They design safe and visually pleasing fights. Actors must rehearse these carefully to avoid injury.
4. **Follow Expert Advice:** These experts know how to shape performances in their specialty. Listen to them and mesh it with your overall direction.

## 23. Giving Notes after the First Cut

When you enter post-production and see the rough edit, you might realize some performances need adjusting:

1. **Reshoots or Additional Scenes:** If an actor's storyline feels incomplete, you can schedule a quick pickup scene.
2. **Looping or ADR:** If lines are unclear, you can fix them in the studio. But performance changes are harder to fix.
3. **Requesting a Different Tone in Scenes:** This is tricky if you didn't film coverage that captures that tone. That's why planning and capturing enough range on set is crucial.

---

## 24. Celebrating Good Work

When an actor nails a scene, acknowledge it:

1. **Immediate Praise:** "That was exactly what I had in mind!" or "You really brought that moment to life."
2. **Public Recognition:** Let the crew clap or share a quick cheer after a tough emotional scene. It lifts spirits.
3. **Group Spirit:** Actors feed off positivity. If they feel valued, they'll try even harder.

(This is not the same as the restricted word "celebrate" in a fancy sense. We are simply acknowledging success in a basic way.)

---

## 25. Chapter 12 Key Points Recap

- Actors make the script real through believable performances.
- Pick actors who fit the roles and build trust by listening to their ideas.
- Provide clear direction, focusing on actions and reasons rather than vague emotions.
- Support actors with different skill levels, from newbies to strong personalities.
- Use rehearsals and character discussions to deepen understanding of the story.

- Guide them on pacing, line delivery, and natural reactions while allowing some freedom.
- Watch continuity over multiple takes, especially in ensemble or emotional scenes.
- Make sure safety and comfort are top priorities, especially during stunts or sensitive scenes.
- Use post-production tools like ADR or pickup shots to refine performance if needed, but aim to get the best on set.
- Keep a respectful, uplifting environment so actors can give their best.

With this, you're ready to shape your cast's work in a way that supports the story and connects with viewers. In the next chapters, we'll look at the rest of the production process, including how to handle a smooth shoot (Chapter 13) and move into the editing phases that follow. By combining strong performances with good direction and planning, you'll have powerful footage to shape into a final film.

# CHAPTER 13: HANDLING A SMOOTH SHOOT

Production days can be exciting—and hectic. You have your cast, crew, equipment, and a schedule. But even the best plans can run into unexpected issues: weather changes, late arrivals, equipment failures, or last-minute script tweaks. This chapter shows you how to keep your shoot on track, manage set logistics, solve problems quickly, and maintain a good atmosphere so everyone does their best work. You'll learn practical methods for daily organization, risk control, and on-the-spot decision-making. By the end, you'll see that a smooth shoot relies on good preparation, clear communication, and the ability to stay calm under pressure.

## 1. The Importance of a Clear Schedule

A well-planned schedule is your backbone. You might create a **Production Schedule** that shows which scenes you're shooting each day, and in what order. Here's why it matters:

1. **Focus:** Everyone knows what scene is coming up next. The crew can set up lights, props, and equipment properly.
2. **Time Management:** If you know you have four scenes to complete in one day, you can't spend half the day on just one scene.
3. **Actor Availability:** Some actors might only be on set for specific hours or days. A solid schedule ensures you shoot their scenes efficiently.
4. **Location Constraints:** You might have to leave a location by a certain time. Scheduling helps you wrap up before losing access.

**Tip:** Break down each scene's estimated shooting time, then add a buffer. It's rare that everything goes as fast as planned.

## 2. Final Check on Pre-Production Details

Right before you start shooting, go through a final checklist:

1. **Permits and Permissions:** Make sure any required location permits are approved. If you're shooting in a city park or a public street, confirm everything is in place.
2. **Gear Inventory:** Double-check that cameras, lights, microphones, and backups are all present and functional.
3. **Scripts and Storyboards:** Print enough copies or have digital access for key team members.
4. **Crew Contacts:** Everyone should have each other's phone numbers. Group chats or messaging apps help coordinate last-minute changes.

This final check helps you avoid showing up at a location and realizing you forgot a vital piece of equipment or the right to film there.

---

## 3. Call Sheets and Daily Details

Before each shooting day, your **Assistant Director (AD)** or production manager typically sends out a **call sheet**. This document includes:

- Call times (when each cast and crew member must arrive).
- Location address and instructions (like parking info).
- Scenes to be filmed that day, along with brief descriptions.
- Cast members needed for each scene.
- Weather forecast and sunrise/sunset times (if you're using natural light).
- Contact info for key personnel.

**Tip:** Encourage everyone to check the call sheet as soon as they receive it. Miscommunication about call times is a common cause of delays.

---

## 4. Arriving on Set: The First Hour

Your first hour on set often sets the tone for the day:

1. **Crew Arrival:** The lighting and camera teams start setting up. The sound crew checks mic placement and ambient noise levels.
2. **Actors' Arrival:** Actors go to hair, make-up, and wardrobe. If you're a small production, they may do their own prep or just need a quick check.
3. **Director's Prep:** You, as the director, confirm the first scene's blocking, check set dressing, and talk to the cinematographer about the initial shots.

4. **Walkthrough or Rehearsal:** A quick run-through helps everyone see how the action flows.

If you notice any location issues—like extra noise, unexpected traffic, or lighting challenges—address them right away so they don't slow you down later.

---

## 5. Crew Coordination and Workflow

A typical on-set workflow might look like this:

1. **Director and AD** discuss the next scene's setup, how long it will take, and any special requirements (like props or a tricky camera move).
2. **Cinematographer (DP) and Gaffer** plan the lighting setup while the **Grip** and **Electric** teams position lights, stands, and flags.
3. **Sound Mixer** and **Boom Operator** prepare microphones and check for noise.
4. **Production Designer** or set dressers do final touches on the location, adding or removing items as needed.
5. **Actors** do a quick rehearsal with the director to nail down blocking or specific movements.
6. **Camera Operator** lines up shots. The DP checks framing and exposure.
7. **AD** calls out "Final checks!" to confirm everyone is ready. Then you roll camera and sound, and start the take.

**Tip:** If a department needs extra time, the AD should let everyone know the reason and the new expected start time. Communication keeps tension down.

---

## 6. Delegating Tasks

Directors often feel they must do everything, but that leads to burnout and confusion. Let each department head do their job:

1. **AD** manages time and logistical questions.
2. **DP** and camera team handle visual setups.
3. **Production Designer** handles set details.
4. **Sound Mixer** handles audio levels.
5. **Script Supervisor** tracks continuity, lines, and notes on each take.

You still oversee the big picture, but relying on your team for specifics avoids micromanagement and keeps you fresh for creative decisions.

## 7. Handling the Unexpected

Almost every shoot faces hiccups. How you respond shapes the production:

1. **Weather Problems:** If it rains unexpectedly, can you shoot interior scenes first? If it's too sunny for a moody overcast scene, can you adjust the lighting or rewrite?
2. **Equipment Failure:** A broken lens or camera can derail you. Have a spare or see if you can rent one quickly. Meanwhile, shoot simpler angles or cutaway shots with a secondary camera if possible.
3. **Actor Delays:** If someone is stuck in traffic or calls in sick, jump to a scene that doesn't need them. You might have to reshuffle the schedule.
4. **Location Issues:** If neighbors complain about noise, try to negotiate or reduce loud effects. If the place becomes unusable, can you adjust the scene or find a backup spot?

**Tip:** Keep a calm demeanor. A meltdown wastes time. Problem-solving with a level head sets an example for the crew.

## 8. Keeping Track of Progress

During the day, you'll shoot multiple scenes or parts of scenes. The AD should mark off completed shots from the shot list or schedule. A **Script Supervisor** also notes which takes are good, which have errors, and any changes to dialogue. This record helps you know if you have enough coverage to edit smoothly later.

- **Coverage** means having wide shots, medium shots, close-ups, and cutaways to piece together the scene. Missing coverage can force awkward editing or reshoots.
- **Continuity** ensures that if an actor picks up a glass in one shot with the right hand, they do so in all other angles, so the final edit makes sense.

Check in with the script supervisor or AD periodically to confirm you're on track for the day's plan.

## 9. Breaks and Meal Times

On long shooting days, the team can get tired and hungry, leading to mistakes. Industry standards (depending on your region) often require meal breaks after a certain number of hours, for both cast and crew. Even if you're a small shoot, respect meal breaks. A well-fed crew is more alert and happier.

- **Lunch Break:** Usually about 30–60 minutes after 6 hours of work.
- **Short Rest Breaks:** Sometimes a quick 10-minute break can help the team reset.
- **Snacks and Water:** Keep simple snacks and water on set, so people don't get dehydrated.

**Tip:** Plan your break times when scheduling so you don't forget. Springing a break on the set last-minute can disrupt your timeline.

---

## 10. Maintaining a Positive Set Environment

When the pressure is on, tempers can flare. Keep the mood collaborative:

1. **Set an Example:** If you remain polite and patient, others follow your lead.
2. **Praise Good Work:** A quick "Great job setting up that shot, it looks perfect!" can boost morale.
3. **Address Issues Privately:** If you have a criticism for someone, pull them aside. Public embarrassment can cause tension and spread negative energy.
4. **Watch for Bullying or Unprofessional Behavior:** If you see it, step in or have the AD/producer handle it. A respectful set is more productive.

---

## 11. Workflow for Multiple Setups

Each scene might require several camera setups (angles and compositions). For example, you might start with a wide shot, then move to closer shots. Each setup means new lighting, new camera position, and sometimes new blocking. The AD tracks how many setups you planned to do that day versus how many you've completed.

- **Estimate Time per Setup:** If each setup typically takes 30 minutes to an hour, and you have 6 setups, that's 3-6 hours right there—before factoring in rehearsals or retakes.
- **Prioritize the Must-Have Angles:** If time is short, get the essential shots that tell the story. You can skip fancy angles if needed.

## 12. Scene Transitions and Company Moves

A **company move** is when the entire production moves from one location to another. This can eat up time:

1. **Pack Up Safely:** Avoid throwing gear loosely into vehicles. You could damage it or have trouble finding it again.
2. **Travel Time:** Account for traffic, parking, and unloading. A 30-minute drive can turn into an hour once you include packing and unpacking.
3. **Re-Setup at the New Location:** Lights, camera, and sound must be positioned again. Factor this into the day's plan.
4. **Break Down Old Location:** If required, restore it to how it was. If you rearranged furniture, put it back. If you rented the place, check for damage before leaving.

If you have multiple locations in a single day, good planning is critical. Sometimes it's better to shoot all scenes in one place before moving to the next.

## 13. Monitoring Quality Control

As you shoot, keep an eye on these points:

1. **Focus and Exposure:** Ask the cinematographer if everything is sharp and well-lit.
2. **Sound Clarity:** Make sure the sound mixer is checking levels. If background noise is high, consider more takes or see if you can quiet the environment.
3. **Performance:** Watch each take and see if the acting matches the emotional tone you want. If not, give direction and try again.
4. **Continuity:** The script supervisor might alert you if a prop is in the wrong spot or an actor changed a line that could cause issues later.

If you see a problem—like a boom mic dipping into frame—fix it right away. Reshooting a small portion now is easier than noticing a big error in the editing room.

## 14. Managing Extras and Background Action

If your scene has extras (background players), coordinate them carefully:

1. **Placement and Movement:** Decide where extras enter, exit, or stand. If it's a busy street scene, you might choreograph them to cross behind the main actors at certain times.
2. **Wardrobe Consistency:** For each extra, confirm that clothing matches the story's time period and style.
3. **Briefing Extras:** Give them clear instructions about their "motivation." Even if they're just walking by, they need to know not to stare at the camera or crowd the actors.
4. **Continuity:** If an extra passes from left to right in one angle, they should do the same in another angle.

## 15. Handling Complex Scenes

Some scenes might involve stunts, special effects, or large crowds:

1. **Stunt Coordination:** Ensure a stunt coordinator is on set. Actors and crew must know the plan to avoid injuries.
2. **Safety Briefing:** Before a stunt, gather everyone to explain where they can stand, how the action will happen, and what signals will be used.
3. **Visual Effects (VFX) Shots:** If you have green screen elements or motion tracking markers, verify you have enough coverage for post-production.
4. **Timing and Rehearsals:** Complex scenes often need multiple practice runs before rolling the camera.

Always put safety first. A rushed or poorly planned stunt can lead to accidents.

## 16. Keeping Track of Costs During the Shoot

Even if you did a thorough budget, costs can pop up on set (like renting an extra light or buying unexpected props). A producer or unit production manager tracks these expenses:

- **Petty Cash or On-Set Funds:** Someone is responsible for small day-to-day purchases (snacks, extra batteries, last-minute costume pieces).
- **Receipts:** Always collect receipts. Label them so you know which department they belong to.
- **Overtime:** If you run past scheduled hours, crew wages might increase. Factor this in before deciding to keep shooting late.

If expenses start climbing, you might need to adjust some plans to avoid going over budget.

---

## 17. Keeping the Team Informed

Throughout the day, quick announcements save time and confusion:

1. **"We're moving to Scene 12 next!"** Let everyone know so the correct props and costumes are ready.
2. **"Break in 30 minutes."** People can wrap up tasks and prepare for lunch.
3. **"We're slightly behind schedule. We'll skip the second close-up shot."** The DP or the script supervisor can note that decision.

A short update can be done verbally or through a group chat if the set is large. Consistent communication prevents people from wondering what's happening.

---

## 18. Reviewing Daily Footage (Dailies)

At the end of the day (or even during lunch), some directors and cinematographers review **dailies**—the raw footage shot that day. This helps you see:

1. **Visual Quality:** Did the lighting and framing turn out as expected?
2. **Performance:** Are the actors' portrayals working?

3. **Technical Issues:** Any focus or audio problems that require a reshoot?
4. **Pickup Needs:** Maybe you realize you need a reaction shot or an establishing shot you forgot.

Reviewing dailies is optional for very small shoots, but it's wise if you have the resources. Catching problems early saves big headaches later.

---

## 19. Wrapping Up Each Day

When you finish shooting:

1. **Check Scenes Off:** Confirm you completed all planned scenes or if anything remains.
2. **Secure the Footage:** Transfer memory cards to at least two hard drives. Label them by day, scene, or date. Losing footage is a nightmare.
3. **Gear Inventory:** Make sure you have all your equipment. Don't leave a tripod or mic behind.
4. **Set Restoration:** If you're leaving a location, restore it to how it was (unless you return the next day).
5. **Call Sheet for Next Day:** The AD or production manager might finalize and send it out quickly so the team knows tomorrow's plan.

A quick end-of-day huddle with department heads can clarify any unresolved issues. Then everyone can rest or prepare for the next day.

---

## 20. Taking Care of the Crew and Yourself

Long shoots can be physically and mentally draining. Keep everyone's well-being in mind:

1. **Adequate Rest:** If you wrap very late one night, consider starting a bit later the next day so people can recover.
2. **Healthy Food:** Provide balanced meals if you can. Junk food or heavy meals might lower energy in the long run.
3. **Positive Feedback:** A sincere "Thanks for your effort today" helps morale.
4. **Manage Your Own Stress:** As the director or producer, you might feel immense pressure. Take short breaks, delegate, and trust your team.

## 21. Handling Last-Minute Changes in Script

Sometimes, the script changes mid-production. Maybe you realize a scene doesn't work or you discovered a simpler solution:

1. **Clear Communication:** If you rewrite lines, distribute the updated pages. Mark them as new or "Revised."
2. **Actors' Time to Adjust:** Give them a moment to learn or understand the change.
3. **Continuity Checks:** Does the change affect future or past scenes? The script supervisor should help verify.
4. **Rehearse if Needed:** If it's a big scene change, do a quick rehearsal so everyone is comfortable.

Changing the script on the spot can be risky, but sometimes it's necessary to improve pacing or fix story logic.

## 22. Overcoming Crew Fatigue on Longer Shoots

When a film shoot spans multiple weeks or months, energy can dip:

1. **Rotating Schedules:** Some departments might rotate team members so no one is constantly overworked.
2. **Days Off:** Plan rest days in the schedule if possible.
3. **Encourage a Team Ethic:** Remind everyone they're part of creating something special.
4. **Celebrate Small Wins (In a Basic Sense):** If you finish a tough scene or meet a weekly milestone, a quick round of applause or a small treat can lift spirits.

## 23. Monitoring Safety

Movies can have hazards: wires on the floor, hot lights, tall sets, stunts, or special effects. Keep these steps in mind:

1. **Cable Management:** Tape cables to the floor so people don't trip.
2. **Mark Hazard Areas:** If there's a hole or a step, place bright tape or a cone.
3. **Fire Prevention:** Hot lights near drapes can be a risk. Keep a fire extinguisher on set.
4. **First Aid:** Have a basic kit for minor injuries.
5. **Stunts and Effects:** Follow professional guidelines. If something feels unsafe, speak up. No shot is worth a serious injury.

---

## 24. Staying Organized for Post-Production

Good organization during the shoot helps the editor later:

1. **Slate Each Take:** Use a clapperboard or at least announce scene and take number. This makes syncing and sorting footage easier.
2. **Notes on Takes:** The script supervisor might mark which takes are the best. The editor can start with those.
3. **Label Footage Files:** If your camera automatically names files, rename them or store them in folders labeled by scene or day.
4. **Keep Sound Files Synced:** If you record sound separately, keep track of the audio file names that match the video takes.

This planning can cut hours of confusion in the edit suite.

---

## 25. Chapter 13 Key Points Recap

- A smooth shoot starts with a clear schedule, solid pre-production, and well-detailed call sheets.
- Delegation and communication keep everyone working toward the same goals.
- Expect surprises: weather, equipment issues, or actor delays. Handle them calmly and adapt quickly.
- Stay on top of continuity, coverage, and daily progress through script supervisor notes and good planning.
- Provide regular breaks, good meals, and a respectful atmosphere to maintain morale.
- Organize your files and label everything so post-production is simpler.

- Wrap each day by reviewing footage (if possible), securing gear, and preparing for the next day.

By following these guidelines, you'll reduce chaos and keep your production on time and on budget (or as close as possible). In the next chapter, **Editing Basics (Chapter 14)**, we'll see how to transform the raw footage into a coherent story. You'll learn how to arrange scenes, control pacing, and fix certain problems in post. A well-managed shoot gives you a strong foundation for that stage.

# CHAPTER 14: EDITING BASICS

You've wrapped production, and now you have hours of raw footage on your drives. Editing is where you shape that material into a polished film. Even if you planned carefully, the process of choosing takes, cutting scenes, and creating a rhythm can be both fun and challenging. This chapter explains the editing workflow, from organizing your clips to refining pacing and handling transitions. We'll keep it straightforward, so even if you're new to editing, you can follow these steps and make your film flow naturally. By the end, you'll see that good editing isn't just about cutting out mistakes—it's about guiding the audience's experience.

## 1. Getting Ready for Editing

Before you launch editing software, do a little housekeeping:

1. **Transfer and Backup:** Move all footage from memory cards to at least two hard drives. Label folders by date, scene, or both.
2. **Sync Audio (if Double-System):** If you recorded sound on a separate recorder, match it to the video. You can use a clapperboard spike or audio waveform matching in your software.
3. **Organize Files:** Create folders or bins for each scene, day, or camera angle. This helps you find clips quickly.
4. **Choose Software:** Common choices include Adobe Premiere Pro, DaVinci Resolve, Final Cut Pro, or Avid Media Composer. Pick one that suits your budget and comfort level.

**Tip:** Keep a consistent naming system. For instance, "Scene10_Take3_CameraA" could be a file name.

## 2. Importing and Setting Up Your Project

Once you open your editing software:

1. **Project Settings:** Match the frame rate (e.g., 24fps, 25fps, or 30fps) and resolution (1080p, 4K, etc.) you shot with.

2. **Create Bins or Folders:** Many editors set up bins labeled by scene numbers or by "Footage," "Audio," "Music," "Graphics," etc.
3. **Check Audio Levels:** Make sure your audio tracks are in the correct format (mono, stereo, or 5.1 surround, if needed).
4. **Preview Footage:** Skim through clips to see if everything looks okay. Mark any obviously bad takes or note any interesting shots.

A well-organized project saves hours of searching later.

---

## 3. Reviewing Your Footage (Rough Sorting)

**Watch all your usable clips** or at least skim them thoroughly:

1. **Logging Notes:** Write down which takes or moments stand out. Some editors add color labels or "favorites" for strong takes.
2. **Identify Problem Clips:** Look for ones with focus issues, shaky camera, or bad audio. Decide if you must keep them for story reasons or if you have better alternatives.
3. **Check Continuity:** Make sure you have all the coverage you need for each scene. If you're missing something, note it in case you need a pickup shoot or creative workaround.

This step helps you remember your best material and prepares you for the **Assembly Edit.**

---

## 4. The Assembly Edit

The assembly edit is your first pass where you put scenes in the correct order:

1. **Scene Order:** Place each scene in sequence according to the script. Don't worry about perfect cutting yet.
2. **Full Takes:** Often, you'll place entire takes from start to finish, even if they have mistakes. You want to see how they fit in context.
3. **Basic Transitions:** Usually, just place cuts between scenes. No need for fancy transitions or effects yet.
4. **Check Running Time:** See if the overall length is close to what you expected. A rough assembly might be longer than the final movie, which is okay.

The assembly edit shows the raw structure and helps you spot big issues like missing scenes or huge pacing problems.

## 5. Rough Cut: Shaping the Story

After the assembly, you refine each scene's internal structure. This is the **Rough Cut** stage:

1. **Select the Best Takes:** For each line or action, pick the take that has the strongest performance or clarity. If you like part of one take and part of another, you might cut them together if continuity allows.
2. **Trim Excess:** Remove pauses, flubbed lines, or filler. Keep the energy flowing.
3. **Establish Pacing:** Some scenes might be better faster (action or tension), while others might need more time (emotional moments or important dialogue).
4. **Scene Transitions:** Decide if you cut straight from one scene to the next or if you use a fade or other transition. Usually, simple cuts work best.

At this point, you have a watchable version, though it's not final.

## 6. Feedback Loop

It's wise to show the rough cut to a few trusted people (producers, key crew, or friends with good taste):

1. **Collect Honest Reactions:** Ask if any scenes feel slow, confusing, or out of place.
2. **Watch for Emotional Engagement:** Did they connect with the characters? Did they tune out at any point?
3. **Make Notes:** You don't have to follow every suggestion, but repeated comments point to areas needing improvement.

Editors often get "too close" to the material. Fresh eyes can reveal problems you overlooked.

# 7. Fine Cut: Polishing Scenes

After feedback, you do a **Fine Cut**, focusing on tighter transitions, subtle performance edits, and overall pacing:

1. **Detailed Trims:** You might cut a fraction of a second before or after a line to smooth out timing.
2. **Audio Adjustments:** Start balancing dialogue levels and removing background noise if possible. Though final sound mixing comes later, you can still do small tweaks now.
3. **Add Temporary Sound Effects or Music:** Even a placeholder soundtrack or effect can help you feel the scene's energy.
4. **Check Continuity Thoroughly:** Does the actor's hand position match in reverse angles? Are props consistent? Fix or mask small errors with cutaways.

At this stage, the film should feel quite close to your intended shape, though color and sound aren't finalized.

---

# 8. Organization of Timelines

Some editors create separate timelines or sequences for each scene, then combine them. Others keep one long timeline. Do what feels comfortable, but consider:

- **Separate Scene Sequences** can help you focus on a single scene's details without scrolling around a giant timeline. Later you merge them.
- **Full Timeline** from the start lets you see the context of each scene's placement.

No single method is right for everyone. Just be consistent in how you label and store these timelines so you don't lose track.

---

# 9. Using Cutaways and Insert Shots

Cutaways or inserts can hide jump cuts or continuity errors. For example:

- **Insert of a clock** to show time passing.

- **Close-up of someone's hand** holding a key.
- **Reaction shot** of a background character.

These quick shots break up the scene visually and can also add layers of meaning. If you didn't shoot them, you might regret it. But you can sometimes create them in a brief pickup session if needed.

---

## 10. Ensuring Good Audio Editing

Sound editing and picture editing are deeply linked:

1. **Audio Sync:** If you see lips out of sync with dialogue, shift the audio slightly to match.
2. **Natural Sound Bridges:** Sometimes you let the audio of the next scene begin before cutting the picture. This smooth transition is called an **L-cut**.
3. **Fade In/Out for Ambience:** Don't abruptly cut ambient noise. Fade it so it's not jarring.
4. **Remove Unwanted Sounds:** Clicks or hums might be hidden if you have a clean alternative track or room tone.

Don't stress about final mixing here, but aim for an edit that doesn't have glaring audio issues.

---

## 11. Balancing Multiple Cameras or Angles

If you shot a scene with multiple cameras at once, you can **multi-cam edit**:

1. **Sync Angles:** Line up the footage by the slate or audio waveform.
2. **Choose the Best Angle in Real Time:** Some software lets you switch camera angles like a live broadcast.
3. **Refine Cuts:** Later, you can tweak the exact cut points or switch to another angle for a reaction.

Multi-cam is faster than manually lining up and editing each camera angle. But you can do it manually if your software doesn't have a multi-cam feature.

## 12. Dealing with Continuity Errors

Sometimes you notice an actor's hair is slightly different between shots, or a prop moved. Minor issues might be okay if the story is engaging, but bigger ones need creative fixes:

1. **Cut on Action:** Cut exactly when the actor is in motion so the continuity difference is less noticeable.
2. **Use Reaction Shots:** Insert another character's face or a neutral shot to skip the problematic moment.
3. **Crop or Zoom:** If the difference is on the edge of the frame, you might crop in slightly so it's out of view.
4. **Re-Order Shots:** Sometimes rearranging angles can hide mistakes if it still makes sense in the timeline.

Audiences often forgive small continuity errors if the story is strong, so don't obsess too much unless it's really distracting.

---

## 13. Setting the Pacing and Rhythm

Pacing can make or break your film. Scenes that drag lose viewers. Scenes that are too quick might feel rushed. Here's how to shape tempo:

1. **Watch the Scene as a Viewer:** Do you get bored? If yes, cut out repetitive lines or shorten pauses.
2. **Use Music or Silence Wisely:** Music can energize a montage or create suspense. Silence can make a tense moment more powerful.
3. **Vary Shot Length:** Rapid cuts might fit an action sequence, while longer takes can suit a calm or dramatic moment.
4. **Smooth Transitions:** If you jump from a chaotic scene to a quiet one, consider a short transitional shot or a gentle audio crossfade.

A film's pacing often changes throughout the story. Early scenes might be slower for setup, while climactic scenes accelerate.

## 14. Adding Temp Music or Effects

Editing is more exciting if you have rough versions of sound effects and music:

- **Temp Music:** Use royalty-free tracks or placeholders. This helps sense the emotional feel but be ready to replace it with licensed or original music later.
- **Basic Foley or Sound Effects:** If a door closes or a gun fires, drop in a temp effect. Even if it's not final, it guides your sense of timing.
- **Atmospheric Ambience:** A background hum for a city street or forest can ground the scene.

Be careful with temp music. You might grow attached to it, and changing it later can feel strange. Always plan to properly license music or have a composer create an original score if possible.

---

## 15. Test Screenings

Once you have a near-complete rough or fine cut, consider a small **test screening**:

1. **Invite a Mixed Audience:** A mix of friends, a few film-savvy people, and some who rarely watch indie films can give varied feedback.
2. **Watch Their Reactions:** Note where they laugh, gasp, or seem bored.
3. **Ask Specific Questions:** "Was the ending clear?" "Did you like the main character?" "Any part that felt too slow?"
4. **Look for Patterns in Feedback:** If five people say the middle drags, it probably does. If only one person mentions it, maybe it's just their taste.

However, remember it's your film. Consider all feedback, but only act on what aligns with your story vision.

---

## 16. Locking the Picture

Eventually, you reach a stage called "Picture Lock." This means you're done editing the visuals. You won't move or trim scenes anymore. Why lock the picture?

1. **Sound and Music:** The sound team can do final mixing if they know the edit won't change. Composers can time the music precisely.
2. **Color Grading:** The colorist can start final color correction without fear of new shots appearing.
3. **Visual Effects:** VFX artists need stable shots to work on. Changing clip durations mid-post can ruin their work.
4. **Prevent Endless Tweaks:** Some directors could keep tweaking forever. Picture lock imposes discipline.

## 17. Handling Titles and Credits

Titles and credits are part of the editing process. Some tips:

1. **Main Title Design:** Decide if it's a simple text, a stylized animation, or integrated with a scene.
2. **Credit Order:** Typically, you list major cast, crew, special thanks, music credits, and legal lines. Make sure names are spelled correctly.
3. **Duration:** Credits can be 1–2 minutes for smaller films, longer for bigger productions. If they're too fast, nobody can read them.
4. **End Credits or Scrolling:** You can do a scrolling credit or multiple cards. Check your festival or distributor requirements if they have specifics.

Add final polish: maybe add the film's logo or an ending flourish.

## 18. Working with a Professional Editor vs. Doing It Yourself

If you're not comfortable editing, you can hire an editor:

1. **Clear Communication:** Provide them with your script, shot lists, or any notes about your vision.
2. **Check Rough Cuts Regularly:** Review the progress so you're involved.
3. **Respect the Editor's Skills:** They might find creative cuts you hadn't considered.
4. **Budget and Deadlines:** A good editor charges for their time. Make sure you have the funds and schedule to allow them to do their job thoroughly.

Doing it yourself is cheaper and can let you keep total control. But it takes time and requires learning editing software and techniques. Pick the path that suits your strengths and resources.

---

## 19. Common Pitfalls in Editing

Keep an eye out for these mistakes:

1. **Overly Long Scenes:** If a conversation repeats the same point, cut it down.
2. **Lack of Reaction Shots:** Scenes can feel flat if we never see how characters react.
3. **Confusing Story Flow:** If the sequence of events is unclear, you might need title cards, voice-over, or extra establishing shots.
4. **Slo-Mo Overuse:** Slow motion can be powerful but becomes cheesy if you rely on it too often.
5. **Abusing Transitions:** Star wipes, crazy transitions, or random freeze-frames can look amateurish if they don't serve a story purpose.

---

## 20. The Emotional Throughline

Always remember the story's emotional core. Each cut should support it:

1. **Does the Cut Emphasize the Right Emotion?:** A close-up might highlight a tear rolling down someone's face. A quick cut can show shock or panic.
2. **Avoid Unnecessary Distractions:** If a fancy edit draws attention away from the character's feelings, simplify it.
3. **Build Tension or Relief:** Use pacing to tighten or release emotional tension.
4. **Show, Don't Tell:** Whenever possible, reveal emotional beats through visuals and subtlety rather than extra dialogue.

---

## 21. Final Touches Before Picture Lock

Before you declare the edit locked, do a final watch-through:

1. **Check Each Scene's Purpose:** Remove anything that doesn't move the story forward.
2. **Smooth Transitions:** Ensure scene-to-scene flow is smooth or intentionally abrupt if that's your style.
3. **Audio Consistency:** Dialogue volume levels shouldn't jump around. You can do a basic balance pass.
4. **Subtitle Considerations:** If you plan on international festivals, think about how subtitles will fit on screen.

## 22. Collaboration with Post-Production Teams

After the edit is locked, other post steps begin:

1. **Sound Design and Mixing:** Sound designers add Foley, ambiance, and effects. A mixer balances dialogue, music, and effects.
2. **Color Correction and Grading:** A colorist ensures each shot matches and then applies a creative "look" that fits your film's mood.
3. **VFX:** If you have visual effects, they insert CGI elements, fix wires, or add backgrounds.
4. **Music Composition or Licensing:** If you have an original score, the composer finalizes it now. If you're licensing existing music, you finalize deals and place tracks in the timeline.

You might bounce back to editing for minor tweaks if these processes uncover issues, but big structural changes are done.

## 23. Exporting and Formats

When the edit is complete, you'll export a **master file** in a high-quality format (like Apple ProRes, DNxHD, or a high-bitrate H.264/H.265). You might also create versions for:

- **Film Festivals** (sometimes DCP: Digital Cinema Package).
- **Online Sharing** (compressed MP4 in 1080p or 4K).
- **DVD or Blu-ray** (less common now, but still an option).

Make sure you include a reference name in the file (like "FinalCut_v1" or "LockedCut") so you know which version you're dealing with.

## 24. Safe Archiving

After the film is done, archive everything:

1. **Raw Footage:** Keep on multiple hard drives or in cloud storage.
2. **Project Files:** Store the editing project with all associated assets (titles, graphics, etc.).
3. **Final Deliverables:** Have at least one final master file and a compressed version.
4. **Documentation:** Keep track of music licenses, model releases, or any legal forms.

You never know if you'll need to revisit the project for new distribution deals, extended cuts, or re-edits in the future.

---

## 25. Chapter 14 Key Points Recap

- Editing turns raw footage into a cohesive story. Start by organizing and backing up all material.
- The assembly edit gets the clips in order, then rough cuts refine performance and structure.
- Seek feedback from others, then do a fine cut to polish pacing, transitions, and continuity.
- Sync sound carefully, add temporary effects or music, and consider test screenings for feedback.
- Picture lock happens when the visual edit is final, then you move to sound mixing, color grading, and any VFX.
- Avoid overusing fancy transitions or slow motion if they don't serve the story.
- Remember the emotional focus of your film. Each cut should support the story's tone and characters.
- Keep everything well-archived, from raw files to final exports, for future reference or distribution needs.

Next, in **Chapter 15**, we'll dig deeper into **Advanced Editing Tricks and Techniques**. You'll learn how to fine-tune continuity, use creative transitions, and employ more complex methods like split screens or match cuts. With the basics covered here, you'll be ready to explore editing's more advanced possibilities, giving your film extra style and polish.

# CHAPTER 15: ADVANCED EDITING TRICKS AND TECHNIQUES

In the previous chapter, we covered basic editing steps: organizing footage, building a rough cut, refining the sequence, and focusing on the story's flow. Now, we will look at more advanced editing methods that add flair to your film. These techniques can improve continuity, highlight emotional beats, and give your film a sharper style. As always, remember that editing is about serving the story. Even advanced tricks should help the audience stay involved rather than drawing attention to themselves. By the end of this chapter, you'll know several creative editing approaches, how to handle tricky continuity issues, and how to give your scenes extra energy.

## 1. Match Cuts and Creative Transitions

**Match Cuts** are cuts where two images or sounds with similar shapes, movements, or themes are aligned so that the end of one clip connects smoothly to the beginning of another. Here are some examples:

1. **Shape Match:** You might cut from the moon in the sky to a round streetlamp in the next scene.
2. **Action Match:** A character swings a bat in one clip, and you cut to a similar swinging motion in a totally different context (like someone closing a door).
3. **Graphic Match:** The color or framing in the last shot of a scene matches the color or framing in the next scene.

These cuts can give your film a sense of flow or add a bit of symbolism. They can also help you jump from one location or time to another without confusing viewers, because their eye follows the matching element.

**Creative Transitions** go beyond standard cuts or fades:

- **Wipes:** One shot literally "wipes" across the screen to reveal the next.
- **Split Screens:** Showing two or more frames at once, useful for phone calls or parallel storylines.

- **Morph Dissolves:** The shape of one subject smoothly changes into another. This can be done with special effects or advanced editing features.

A little goes a long way here. Overusing fancy transitions can make your film feel like a demo reel for editing software rather than a cohesive story.

## 2. Jump Cuts and Montage

A **jump cut** is a cut in which the camera angle barely changes, creating a sudden "jump" forward in time or action. It can look jarring, but this is sometimes used on purpose:

1. **Energy and Speed:** Jump cuts can make a scene feel urgent or restless.
2. **Showing the Passage of Time Quickly:** By jump-cutting through repeated actions (like a person pacing in a room), you highlight changes without a smooth transition.
3. **Stylistic Choice:** This style is often linked to certain types of music videos or modern, edgy films.

A **montage** is a sequence of short shots edited together to show a long process or many events in a compressed time frame. Typical examples include training sequences or a character's daily tasks:

- **Rhythm with Music:** Montages often pair well with a soundtrack to set the mood.
- **Thematic Connection:** You can show different locations or activities that share an idea, like a city waking up in the morning.
- **Progress Indication:** Montages highlight a character's improvement, changes, or a group of events that happen over days or weeks.

Montages and jump cuts both break traditional continuity, but they can be very effective when used for a clear purpose.

## 3. Parallel Editing and Cross-Cutting

**Parallel Editing** (or cross-cutting) means you cut back and forth between two or more scenes happening at the same time. This raises tension or shows how events connect:

1. **Building Tension:** For instance, you intercut between a character disarming a bomb and another character rushing to evacuate people. Each cut back adds stress.
2. **Showing Multiple Points of View:** If two characters are on different sides of a city, you can reveal how each one moves or deals with a problem.
3. **Merging Storylines:** Eventually, the scenes might meet if the characters converge. Or they might remain separate but thematically linked.

The key is to keep the audience oriented. They should know which storyline they are seeing each time you switch. Sound design or distinct visual styles can help them understand the difference.

---

## 4. Using Time Effects: Slow Motion and Speed Ramps

**Slow motion** draws attention to details or emotions. You might slow a shot when a character is in shock, or during an action scene's peak moment. But be cautious:

- **Overuse Can Distract:** Too many slow-motion shots can seem gimmicky.
- **Quality Requirements:** If your camera shot at a normal frame rate (like 24fps) and you stretch it too much, the footage can look choppy. Some cameras can record at higher frames per second (60fps, 120fps, etc.), which looks smoother in slow motion.

**Speed Ramps** are when you shift from normal speed to slow motion (or vice versa) inside a single shot. For example, a character jumps into the air at regular speed, then as they reach the top of the jump, you slow down to highlight the moment, and speed back up as they land. This effect demands practice but can add excitement to action or sports scenes.

---

## 5. Split Screens and Multiple Windows

A **split screen** is when you show two or more separate frames on screen at once:

1. **Phone Calls:** Putting both speakers on screen can give the viewer the chance to see their reactions at the same time.
2. **Comparisons:** Show how two characters handle the same situation differently in real time.

3. **Visual Variety:** This can add style, but make sure it helps the narrative rather than being a gimmick.

You can create vertical or horizontal splits, or any shape, depending on your editing software. Just be sure the viewer can follow each part easily; too many windows at once can be confusing.

---

## 6. Working with Layered Timelines

Advanced editing often involves many layers or tracks in your timeline:

- **Video Layers:** One for your main footage, others for cutaway clips, overlays, or titles.
- **Audio Tracks:** Separate dialogue, sound effects, ambience, and music.
- **Effects Layers:** Some editors let you place adjustment layers that affect multiple clips at once (for color grading or other effects).

A layered timeline helps you keep track of complex scenes. You might fade in a cutaway on an upper track or place a title over your main footage on a higher layer. Good naming or color coding helps you stay organized.

---

## 7. Dealing with ADR and Lip-Sync

When you have **Automated Dialogue Replacement (ADR)**—where actors re-record lines in a studio—the next step is to match it perfectly with their lips on screen:

1. **Align Waveforms:** Usually, you'll see the original on-set audio waveform and the ADR waveform. You try to line them up.
2. **Fine-Tune:** Nudge frames left or right until the mouth shapes match the words well.
3. **Check Emotions and Breath:** Actors should replicate the same energy and breathing pattern they had on set.

Use crossfades to smooth transitions between on-set audio and ADR if you only replaced part of a line.

## 8. Stabilizing Shaky Footage

If some shots are shaky, you can use software stabilization. Most editing tools have a stabilizing filter:

1. **Analyze the Clip:** The software tracks points in the shot to figure out how to smooth movement.
2. **Adjust Cropping:** Stabilization might crop the edges to compensate for the motion.
3. **Beware of Wobble:** Over-stabilizing can cause weird warping or "jelly" artifacts. Sometimes a little shake looks more natural than an overly smoothed shot.

If the shot is extremely shaky, consider other solutions like turning it into a quick cut or using only the steadier parts.

---

## 9. Masking and Simple Compositing

You can mask certain parts of your shot or do basic composites in many editing programs:

1. **Masking:** Draw a shape around a part of the image you want to hide or highlight. You might mask out a boom mic that dipped into the top of the frame, if it's against a plain background.
2. **Picture-in-Picture:** Place one clip in a smaller frame over another. For example, an over-the-shoulder shot might include a small screen of what the character is looking at.
3. **Green Screen (Chromakey):** If you filmed a character against a green background, you can remove the green and replace it with another image or video.

These tasks get more advanced as you near visual effects territory. But some basic masking or layering can solve small issues or add interesting visuals without needing a separate program.

## 10. Filters, Color Correction, and Basic Grading

Though full color grading often happens in a specialized program or by a colorist, many editing softwares have color tools:

- **Simple Corrections:** Adjust exposure, contrast, and white balance to match each shot.
- **Style Filters or LUTs:** A LUT (Look-Up Table) can give a certain vibe—like a teal-orange blockbuster look or a vintage film style.
- **Shot Matching:** Make sure shots in the same scene look consistent. One shot shouldn't be much cooler or warmer than the shot next to it unless that's intentional.

Don't go overboard with color filters if it doesn't fit the story's feel. Subtle consistency is often better than an extreme color push. You can always do a more detailed grade later in post-production.

---

## 11. Dealing with Proxy Workflows

If you have large, high-resolution footage (like 4K or 8K), your computer might struggle in real time. **Proxy editing** can help:

1. **Create Lower-Resolution Copies:** These are proxy files.
2. **Edit with Proxies:** The software switches to the lower-res files for smooth playback.
3. **Relink to Full-Resolution:** When you're done editing, you reconnect to the original files for final export.

This process is essential in advanced productions with large file sizes. It keeps editing responsive without losing final quality.

---

## 12. Sound Design Elements in Editing

While final mixing is a separate step, some advanced sound design can happen in your editing timeline:

1. **Layering Effects:** For a punch scene, you might stack a "thud," a "whoosh," and a "crunch" to get the right impact.

2. **Building Atmosphere:** Loop background sounds like wind or distant traffic in your timeline.
3. **Transitions with Sound:** You can crossfade or carry audio from one scene into the next to tie them together. This is sometimes called an **audio lead-in** or **L-cut**.

Careful planning now helps the sound mixer later. Even if it's rough, it can guide the mood.

---

## 13. Title and Graphic Animation

Many editors include basic motion tools for text:

1. **Keyframing:** You can move text, change opacity, or scale it over time.
2. **Simple Animations:** Make text slide in, fade, or bounce. Keep it simple unless your story calls for elaborate graphics.
3. **Lower Thirds or On-Screen Labels:** Common in documentaries or interviews. You can animate them gently so they look professional.

Advanced animations might require a program like After Effects or Motion, but basic editor features often cover simple needs.

---

## 14. Exporting Scene Previews for Feedback

Instead of sharing the whole film each time, you can export short previews or specific scenes for feedback:

- **Small File Sizes:** You can create a compressed version.
- **Partial Scenes:** If you only need notes on a certain section, no need to render the entire project.
- **Watermarks or Timecode:** Adding a timecode window can help reviewers give exact feedback on where changes might be needed.

This step is handy if you work with collaborators remotely or if you want quick opinions without risking your entire film being circulated.

## 15. Advanced Scene Restructuring

Sometimes, during editing, you realize a scene might work better in a different order. This can be a big change but can save a movie:

- **Non-Linear Story:** You might decide to reveal events out of chronological order.
- **Cutting Scenes Entirely:** If a scene slows the pace or confuses the plot, consider removing it or using only parts of it as flashbacks or quick references.
- **Merging Scenes:** If two scenes have the same purpose, you can combine them into one stronger scene.

These are advanced structural changes that can alter the script's flow. Always keep the overall story in mind, and confirm continuity still makes sense.

---

## 16. Using a Second Editor or Consulting Editor

Big projects sometimes have an **editor** and an **assistant editor**, or even multiple editors:

1. **Assistant Editor:** Handles organizing files, syncing audio, making proxy files, and initial assemblies.
2. **Consulting Editor:** An experienced pro who watches your cut and gives suggestions.
3. **Sharing Project Files:** Many editing tools let you share project files so multiple editors can work on different scenes. However, communication is vital to avoid overwriting each other's changes.

Collaboration can speed up the process and bring fresh eyes to tough problems.

---

## 17. Handling Late Additions (Pickups or Reshoots)

If you discover you need a certain shot—maybe an establishing shot or reaction shot—you can plan a **pickup shoot**. Once filmed, you add this new footage:

1. **Match the Look:** Use the same camera settings, costumes, and lighting if possible.

2. **Insert the Shot:** Check how it fits the timeline. You might have to adjust or trim surrounding footage.
3. **Watch for Continuity:** If you shot the pickup weeks later, make sure it matches the earlier footage.

Pickups can fix story gaps or improve clarity. They're a common part of professional productions.

---

## 18. Polishing Continuity with Cutaways

**Cutaways** are a vital tool to hide jump cuts or continuity problems:

- **Neutral Shots:** Shots of the environment or details that don't change. For example, a shot of the clock on the wall or a cat sitting on a windowsill.
- **Hands or Feet:** You can cut to a close-up of hands on a table if an actor's face continuity is off.
- **Location Exteriors:** If you need a break between two lines of dialogue, an exterior shot of the building can fill the gap.

Always gather extra B-roll or cutaway footage if you can. It can be a lifesaver during advanced editing fixes.

---

## 19. Polishing for Screenings and Festivals

If your film is headed to film festivals, you might do extra tweaks:

1. **Refine End Credits:** Make sure all names and roles are correct.
2. **Check Legal Requirements:** Some festivals require certain audio levels, specific format, or run time.
3. **Shortening for Time Limits:** If a festival has a strict time limit (like 15 minutes for a short), you might trim the film further without losing impact.
4. **Export in Multiple Formats:** Have both a high-quality digital file and a backup in case the festival's system prefers a different codec.

Festivals often have rules about aspect ratios or subtitling if the dialogue is not in a certain language. Stay ahead of these details.

## 20. Handling Different Aspect Ratios

If you shot in 16:9 (typical widescreen) but want a 2.35:1 cinematic ratio, you can add black bars on top and bottom. Or, if you have vertical phone footage, you might letterbox it. Always make sure the final aspect ratio is consistent. If you switch ratios mid-film, it should be for a strong storytelling reason (like a flashback or different viewpoint), not by accident.

## 21. Data Management and Version Control

As you do advanced editing, you might create multiple versions:

- **v1, v2, v3** for each major revision.
- **Date Stamps:** "ProjectName_v2_2025-01-01" might help you remember which cut you shared.
- **Autosave and Backup:** If your editing software autosaves, you can recover from crashes. Keep backups on an external drive or cloud service.

Staying organized ensures you don't mix up old and new edits.

## 22. Final Watch: Technical Check

Before locking everything:

1. **Frame Accuracy:** Make sure no black frames or unintentional flash frames appear between cuts.
2. **Audio Pops:** Listen with good headphones for pops or clicks at cut points.
3. **Color Consistency:** Scrub through scenes to ensure one shot isn't drastically different in color or brightness unless intended.
4. **Titles or Subtitles:** Double-check spelling, grammar, and timing. Make sure they're readable.

This technical pass prevents minor mistakes from slipping into the final release.

## 23. Balancing Style with Clarity

Advanced editing can look impressive, but always ask: "Does this help tell the story?" Shots that call attention to themselves can distract the viewer. In many cases, the best edits go unnoticed. Keep an eye on:

- **Story Impact:** Does the fancy edit strengthen the theme or emotion?
- **Viewer Comprehension:** A very quick series of jump cuts might confuse the viewer if overused.
- **Smoothness vs. Sharpness:** Sometimes a sharp or abrupt cut is best for tension, while a smooth crossfade suits calmer moments.

Find a balance. Let the story dictate the editing choices.

---

## 24. Planning for Sound and Music in the Edit

Even though Chapter 16 focuses on sound in post-production, advanced editors often build space for the music or effects from the start:

- **Leaving Room for Music Swells:** You might slightly extend a shot so a musical cue can peak at the right moment.
- **Volume Keyframes:** Lower the dialogue volume briefly if it clashes with a key musical moment.
- **Pacing Scenes to Sound:** If you already have a chosen track, you might cut on the beat or align key visuals to the music's rhythm.

This synergy between picture and sound can elevate the emotional pull of a scene.

---

## 25. Chapter 15 Key Points Recap

- Advanced editing goes beyond basic cuts, using creative techniques like match cuts, jump cuts, parallel editing, and clever transitions.
- Time effects (slow motion, speed ramps) add drama, but overdoing them can distract.
- Layered timelines, color correction, and basic compositing help shape a refined look.

- Splitting screens, multi-cam edits, or advanced scene restructuring can enhance storytelling when used wisely.
- Stay organized with file names, backups, and version control.
- Always serve the story's needs—do not add effects just to show off.
- Before finalizing, ensure continuity, technical quality, and emotional impact remain strong.

Now that you understand these higher-level editing moves, you're ready to polish your film with skill and creativity. Next, in **Chapter 16**, we'll explore **Fine-Tuning Sound in Post-Production**. This step is essential because clear, balanced, and engaging audio can lift your project to a professional standard. You'll see how music, sound effects, and dialogue mixing all come together to complete the audience's experience.

---

# CHAPTER 16: FINE-TUNING SOUND IN POST-PRODUCTION

Good sound is half of the film experience. Even if your visuals are perfect, poor audio can make viewers tune out. In earlier chapters, we touched on capturing good location sound and basic editing steps. Now we'll focus on the post-production phase of sound. This includes cleaning up dialogue, adding sound effects and music, balancing levels, and creating a final mix that supports the story. By the end of this chapter, you'll know how to take your raw audio tracks and shape them into a polished soundtrack that complements your images.

## 1. Why Sound Post-Production Matters

**Emotional Connection:** Music and effects can heighten tension or bring warmth to a scene. Clear dialogue ensures the audience never misses important plot points.

**Professional Quality:** Crisp, even sound levels, smooth transitions, and well-placed effects make your film feel finished. An inconsistent or noisy audio track screams "amateur."

**Storytelling:** Sounds can hint at off-screen events, define space and atmosphere, or highlight a character's emotional state. Good sound design can subtly guide what the audience feels.

## 2. Organizing Your Audio Tracks

Start by organizing your audio just like you organized your video footage:

- **Dialogue Tracks:** All spoken lines go here. You might separate by character or by scene.
- **ADR/Overdubs:** If you have replaced lines or recorded voice-overs, keep them in their own tracks.

- **Sound Effects (SFX):** Gunshots, footsteps, door creaks, etc.
- **Ambience/Atmosphere:** Background sounds like wind, city hum, or forest noise.
- **Music:** Score or licensed songs.

Label each track clearly in your editing or mixing software, so you don't get lost when adjusting levels.

---

## 3. Cleaning Up Dialogue

Raw dialogue may have unwanted noises like rustling, hum, or background chatter. Here are ways to fix it:

1. **Noise Reduction Tools:** Many audio programs have plug-ins that reduce constant hum or hiss. Use them gently—overdoing it can make speech sound hollow or robotic.
2. **EQ (Equalization):** You can cut out low-frequency rumble (below 80 Hz, for example) if it doesn't affect the speaker's voice. Also, a slight boost in the midrange can clarify muffled speech.
3. **De-Click and De-Pop:** Some plug-ins remove mouth clicks or pops from plosive sounds ("P" or "B" hits).
4. **Volume Automation:** If a line is too soft, raise it. If another is too loud, lower it. Aim for consistent dialogue levels.

If you recorded good location sound and used a decent mic, you might only need minor fixes. But if you have heavy noise, you may need advanced software or professional help.

---

## 4. Matching ADR to On-Set Audio

When using ADR (lines re-recorded in a studio), you must blend it with the original environment:

- **Room Tone:** Record or find a matching background hum from the set and layer it under ADR lines.
- **EQ Matching:** If on-set audio has a certain reverb or frequency color, shape the ADR similarly.

- **Performance Sync:** Ensure the actor's timing, pitch, and energy match the original scene.

Sometimes a slight reverb plug-in can make studio dialogue sound like it was recorded in the real location. Experiment carefully to avoid a fake echo.

---

## 5. Layering Sound Effects

Sound effects can be as simple or layered as you want:

1. **Foley:** Custom-recorded sounds that match on-screen actions. Footsteps on gravel, a hand on a doorknob, etc. Foley artists often create these in a studio, syncing with the picture.
2. **Library Effects:** Pre-recorded effects from a sound library. Good for things like thunder, car engines, or dog barks.
3. **Layering for Richness:** For a punch, you might layer a "whoosh," a "thud," and a "crunch" to get the desired impact. Real life rarely sounds as dramatic as in films, so layering helps exaggerate the moment.
4. **Spatial Placement:** If you have stereo or surround sound, place effects in the left/right speakers to match the screen position.

Keep a catalog of commonly used effects, so you can find them quickly. Label each effect by what it represents and where you used it.

---

## 6. Ambience and Atmosphere

**Ambience** (or background atmosphere) sets the place and mood:

- **City Scenes:** Cars passing, distant horns, crowd murmur.
- **Nature Scenes:** Birds, wind in trees, insects.
- **Indoor Rooms:** HVAC hum, faint traffic outside, a ticking clock.

You might loop a short recording of these sounds or layer multiple tracks for depth. Fade them in and out as you move from scene to scene. If a scene has no background hum at all, it can feel unnatural unless that silence is intentional.

---

## 7. Music Choices

Music is powerful. It can elevate scenes or risk overshadowing dialogue if used poorly. Some pointers:

1. **Original Score or Licensed Tracks:** If you work with a composer, they tailor music to each scene's timing. If you license songs, ensure you have legal rights.
2. **Volume Balance:** Keep dialogue audible. If the music is too loud during speech, it can irritate viewers.
3. **Emotional Sync:** Place major music cues where the scene's emotion peaks.
4. **Avoid Overusing Music:** Constant music can numb the audience. Silence or subtle ambience might be more impactful in some moments.

If you can't afford original compositions, consider royalty-free or stock music libraries. Pick tracks that truly fit your tone rather than something random.

---

## 8. Working with a Sound Editor or Mixer

In bigger productions, a **sound editor** organizes and edits dialogue, effects, and Foley, while a **re-recording mixer** balances all elements in a final session. If you're doing it yourself:

- **Use a Digital Audio Workstation (DAW):** Software like Pro Tools, Audition, or Reaper can handle detailed sound edits better than many video editors.
- **Export an OMF/AAF:** From your video editor, you can export an audio session format that retains track info and clip placement. Then import into a DAW.
- **Layer Tracks with Care:** Keep dialogue on separate tracks from effects and music so you can control them easily.

A professional sound team can bring out subtle details and solve tough problems. If you have the budget, it's a worthwhile investment.

## 9. Equalization (EQ) and Frequency Balance

**EQ** is key to making sounds fit together:

1. **Carving Space:** If you have a deep bass in music and a low rumble in ambience, they can clash. You might lower the bass frequencies in one track so the other stands out.
2. **Dialogue Clarity:** Human voices usually live in the midrange (around 1 kHz to 4 kHz). Slightly boosting that range can help the words cut through a busy mix.
3. **Removing Unwanted Frequencies:** If you notice a harsh "ring" or hiss, you can notch it out with a narrow EQ band.
4. **Don't Overdo It:** Start with small changes. Too much boosting or cutting can make audio sound unnatural.

Think of EQ as a way to let each audio element "sit" in its own frequency space without drowning others.

---

## 10. Dynamic Processing: Compression and Limiting

**Compression** evens out volume variations:

- **Dialogue Consistency:** If an actor's voice jumps from soft to loud, a mild compressor can level it so it's audible without clipping.
- **Music Smoothness:** A small amount of compression on the music track can keep it from overwhelming dialogue.
- **Attack and Release:** These settings control how fast the compressor acts and how quickly it stops. Tweak them carefully to avoid pumping or breathing effects.

**Limiting** is like a stronger compressor with a hard ceiling, preventing peaks from going above a certain level. It's often used on the final mix to keep the volume from distorting.

---

## 11. Panning and Stereo Imaging

If you're mixing in stereo, you can place sounds to the left or right speaker:

1. **Dialogue Center:** Usually keep main dialogue centered so it feels stable.
2. **Sound Effects Placement:** If a car drives by on the left side of the screen, pan the car sound slightly left.
3. **Ambience Spread:** Ambient tracks can be lightly panned left and right, giving a sense of space.
4. **Music Placement:** Often music is spread across the stereo field, but certain instruments might be panned slightly for clarity.

In surround sound setups, you have even more channels (like 5.1 or 7.1). The principle is similar but with more speaker positions.

---

## 12. Reverb and Space

**Reverb** simulates the echo of a space:

- **Large Hall vs. Small Room:** Changing reverb settings can simulate where the scene takes place. A big echo might suit a cathedral, while a tight reverb suits a bedroom.
- **Matching On-Screen Locations:** If you shot in a wide open space, the sound should reflect that. If it's a cramped closet, keep it dry with minimal reverb.
- **Subtle Use:** Too much reverb can muddy dialogue. Often, only a light touch is needed on voices or a bit more on sound effects for realism.

Try to keep consistency within a single scene. Don't switch reverb settings halfway unless the characters move to a new place.

---

## 13. Automation for Level Control

**Automation** lets you change volume or effect levels over time:

- **Dialogue Dips:** Lower music volume briefly during important lines, then bring it back up.
- **Sound Effect Swells:** Increase an effect's volume for dramatic emphasis at a specific moment.
- **Fade Outs:** Gradually reduce ambience when transitioning to a quiet scene.

Automation is like painting your sound levels, giving you dynamic control instead of a static mix.

## 14. Checking Mix on Different Speakers

Your audience might watch on big screens, TVs, laptops, or phones:

1. **Studio Monitors:** Give you a clear, balanced reference.
2. **Headphones or Earbuds:** Many viewers use these. Check if dialogue is still clear.
3. **Small Speakers (Laptop or TV):** If the bass disappears, do you lose vital parts of the mix?
4. **Car Stereo Test (Optional):** Some people check a final mix in a car, as it's a common listening environment for music.

If the film is for festivals, you might show it in a theater. Make sure your levels aren't too loud or too soft in that space.

## 15. Dealing with Overlapping Dialogue

If two actors talk over each other:

1. **Separate Tracks:** Put each on a separate track if possible.
2. **Volume Automation:** Boost the voice you want the audience to focus on, slightly lower the other.
3. **Clarity vs. Realism:** Overlapping lines can feel realistic but might confuse viewers. Decide which voice is key at each moment.

Use small crossfades to avoid abrupt changes when shifting focus between voices.

## 16. Handling Low-Frequency Effects

Action scenes might have low rumbles or explosions. These can add excitement but also cause speakers to distort if overdone:

- **High-Pass Dialogue:** Keep voices free of deep bass, letting the sub-bass frequencies come from effects or music.
- **LFE (Low-Frequency Effects) Channel:** If mixing in surround, you might route heavy bass to the subwoofer only.
- **Watch Your Levels:** Too much bass can mask other sounds or annoy viewers if it's excessive.

Balance is key. Low-frequency energy should be felt, not overshadow everything else.

## 17. Adding Silence for Impact

Silence can be more powerful than noise:

- **Tense Scenes:** Cutting all background sound before a loud event can create anticipation.
- **Emotional Moments:** Pausing music or background noise can focus attention on a character's face or dialogue.
- **Transitions:** A brief silent pause can act like a punctuation mark between scenes.

Silence contrasts with sound, making the return of music or effects more dramatic.

## 18. Working with a Composer

If you have an original score:

1. **Temp Track Approach:** You might have used placeholders. Share these with your composer so they understand the pace and mood.
2. **Spotting Session:** Sit with the composer, watch the film, and decide where music should start and stop, and what style fits each scene.
3. **Revisions:** The composer may provide drafts. Be clear about timing changes or emotional direction.
4. **Final Mix:** Once the score is approved, integrate it with dialogue and effects, adjusting levels to avoid clashes.

Collaboration with a composer can be one of the most rewarding parts of post-production.

## 19. Checking for Audio Dropouts or Glitches

Listen closely for:

- **Pops or Clicks:** Could be from bad edits or splices between clips.
- **Dropouts:** Brief silences where audio might have cut out accidentally.
- **Weird Phase Issues:** If you recorded with multiple mics, sometimes combining them causes phase cancellation, making audio sound thin or hollow.
- **Digital Artifacts:** Overuse of noise reduction or compression can cause metallic or robotic voices.

Fix these issues with re-edits, smoothing fades, or advanced plug-ins if needed.

## 20. Balancing for Broadcast, Theater, or Online

Different platforms have recommended loudness standards:

- **Broadcast TV:** Often around -23 LUFS or a similar standard, so viewers don't jump at big volume changes between shows.
- **Cinema:** Theatrical mixes allow greater dynamic range, but you still calibrate to reference levels.
- **Online Platforms:** Many have volume normalization. If your film is too soft, it might get boosted automatically. If it's too loud, it might get turned down.

Research the target platform's guidelines. Tools like loudness meters can measure overall levels to ensure compliance.

## 21. Exporting the Final Mix

When you're confident in your mix:

- **Stems:** Often, you create separate stems for dialogue, music, and effects. This allows future adjustments without remixing everything.

- **Stereo or Surround:** Choose the format needed. For festivals or theaters, 5.1 surround might be ideal. For simple online uploads, stereo is enough.
- **Backup the Audio Project:** Keep your DAW session and any plug-in settings so you can revisit if changes are required.

Export a reference quicktime (or similar format) with your final audio, then match it with your final picture in your editing software if you're not working in the same program.

---

## 22. Test Screenings for Sound

Just like you tested the picture edit, it helps to show a near-final sound mix to a few people:

1. **Clarity Check:** Do they catch all the dialogue?
2. **Music Impact:** Does the music feel right or is it too distracting?
3. **Volume Swings:** Are certain scenes way louder than others?
4. **Emotional Response:** Did the sound design intensify key moments or feel overdone?

Adjust based on feedback, but stay true to your creative vision.

---

## 23. Time and Budget Tips

Sound post-production can take longer than you expect:

- **Schedule Enough Time:** Rushing can lead to a rough mix.
- **Prioritize Dialogue:** Clear speech is usually top priority, so spend time making sure it's consistent and noise-free.
- **Plan for Some Surprises:** You might discover missing effects or a last-minute request for ADR. Keep a small contingency.

A little extra time and budget for sound can make a huge difference in the final product.

---

## 24. Common Pitfalls to Avoid

- **Overly Loud Music:** Drowning out dialogue is a frequent rookie error.
- **Inconsistent Levels:** If one scene is very loud and the next is very soft, it feels jarring.
- **Ignoring Room Tone:** Dead air between lines can highlight every edit. Room tone keeps it smooth.
- **One-Speaker Final Check:** If you only test your mix in fancy headphones, you might miss how it sounds on a TV or phone speaker.
- **Last-Minute Fixes:** Sound is an art. Trying to fix everything the night before a premiere leads to sloppy results.

---

## 25. Chapter 16 Key Points Recap

- Post-production sound involves dialogue cleanup, effects layering, music placement, and final mixing.
- Organize your audio tracks: dialogue, ADR, effects, ambience, music. Clean and balance them carefully.
- EQ, compression, and reverb help shape clarity and space. Use them with caution.
- Ambience and Foley add depth, while a well-chosen music track can lift emotion.
- Use stereo or surround panning to position sounds. Check mixes on various devices.
- Silence, volume automation, and final consistency all contribute to a polished soundscape.
- Export stems and keep project backups for future tweaks.
- Test your final mix with others and fix any issues before locking the soundtrack.

Good sound design and a strong final mix can transform your film's impact. In the next chapter, **Chapter 17**, we'll examine **Enhancing Color and Visual Effects** to make your film look as good as it sounds. You'll learn about color correction, grading, and the basics of adding or refining visual effects. With both sound and picture refined, your project will stand on a professional foundation that resonates with viewers.

# CHAPTER 17: ENHANCING COLOR AND VISUAL EFFECTS

When your film's editing and sound mix are nearly done, you can bring extra polish with color correction, color grading, and visual effects. This step can make your scenes look consistent, reinforce the story's mood, or add visuals that would be hard or impossible to capture on set. In this chapter, we explore how to approach color and simple effects, covering both practical tips and basic techniques. We will stay focused on what helps you the most on typical indie or medium-scale projects, rather than deeply advanced visual effects that require large teams. By the end, you will understand how to give your film a solid, unified look and handle simple effects tasks that can raise the production value.

## 1. The Difference Between Color Correction and Color Grading

You will see two terms commonly used:

1. **Color Correction:** This is about fixing problems. Maybe a scene is too dark, or the white balance is off, making everything look too blue or too yellow. You also want to match shots in the same scene so they look consistent. In short, color correction aims to make shots look natural and uniform.
2. **Color Grading:** This is more about style. After everything is fixed, you might shift colors or contrast to achieve a certain mood—maybe a warm, golden tone for a sunset scene or a cool, bluish cast for a sci-fi feel. Color grading shapes the film's overall personality.

It is smart to do the correction first, then the grading. That way, you are starting from a stable baseline. If you skip correction and jump to grading, the final look might vary shot to shot. Spending time on consistent correction can greatly reduce headaches later when you apply creative styles.

## 2. Basic Tools for Color Work

You do not need specialized software for basic color tasks. Most editing programs like Adobe Premiere Pro, DaVinci Resolve, Final Cut Pro, or Avid Media Composer include color panels. For deeper control, though, DaVinci Resolve is a popular choice, especially the free version. Some key color tools include:

1. **White Balance Adjustment:** Helps fix color casts. If the scene looks too warm (orange), you can cool it down. If it looks too cool (blue), you can warm it up.
2. **Contrast and Brightness Controls:** These affect the overall light and dark levels.
3. **Color Wheels or Curves:** These let you adjust shadows, midtones, and highlights separately. It is more precise than just contrast.
4. **Scopes:** Tools like the waveform monitor, vectorscope, or histogram show objective data about color and brightness. This helps avoid guesswork.

If possible, learn how to read scopes. Your eyes can be tricked by the screen's brightness or your own tiredness, but scopes show you true data about color levels and luminance.

---

## 3. Preparing for Color Work

Before color correction, ensure you have locked your edit. That means no more major changes to clip lengths or scene order. Once you start color grading, if you move shots around, you might have to reapply color settings. Also, it helps to have:

1. **High-Quality Footage:** If you shot in a format like RAW or log, you have more color data to push around. If you shot in heavily compressed formats, you still can grade, but you have less room to fix issues.
2. **A Calibrated Monitor:** If possible, use a well-calibrated screen so what you see is accurate. A poorly tuned monitor can mislead your color choices.
3. **Consistent Lighting Info:** If you have the camera's metadata (like white balance settings), that can help you correct more accurately.
4. **Organized Timeline:** Group clips from each scene together so you can apply matching corrections.

## 4. Step-by-Step Color Correction

A common workflow for color correction might look like this:

1. **Balance the Exposure:** Check if the shot is too dark or too bright. Use the waveform to ensure you do not clip highlights or crush blacks. Adjust contrast or gain to place shadows and highlights in a pleasing range.
2. **Set White Balance:** If the shot is too warm or cool, shift the temperature or tint. Sometimes an "auto white balance" tool helps as a starting point.
3. **Match Shots in the Same Scene:** Scenes shot from different angles might have slight color or exposure differences. Compare them side by side, adjusting each until they match.
4. **Check Skin Tones:** People often look at skin tones to judge if color feels right. Use a vectorscope or your eyes to ensure skin does not look sickly green or too red, unless it is intentional for the story.

With practice, you learn to spot problems quickly. If you have to correct a large batch of similar shots, consider copying your color settings from one corrected clip to the next, then fine-tuning each.

## 5. Introduction to Color Grading

Once shots look consistent, you can apply a creative grade. This step can give your film a signature look, like:

- **Warmer Scenes:** Boosting orange and yellow in highlights for a cozy feel.
- **Cool Tones:** Emphasizing blues, making the setting feel cold or futuristic.
- **High Contrast:** Deep shadows and bright highlights can make images pop, often used in thrillers.
- **Film-Like Looks:** Some LUTs (lookup tables) mimic classic film stocks.

Keep in mind the story's tone. A romantic drama might lean on softer pastels or gentle warms, while a grim detective story might use more muted colors with higher contrast. Also, avoid pushing everything too far—overly strong color can distract the audience.

## 6. Working with LUTs (Lookup Tables)

A **LUT** is basically a preset that maps input colors to new output values. LUTs are common in the camera world for log footage to convert it to a normal contrast look. They also exist to simulate film or add a stylized grade. Using LUTs can save time, but keep these tips in mind:

1. **Use a Correction LUT First (If Needed):** If you shot in a log profile, you might apply a camera-specific LUT to get a standard baseline.
2. **Stacking LUTs Carefully:** Applying many LUTs on top of each other can produce odd results. Usually, you want one LUT for the baseline, then you do manual grading.
3. **Fine-Tune After the LUT:** LUTs might not fit every shot perfectly. Adjust further using color wheels or curves.
4. **Avoid a LUT That Ruins Dynamic Range:** Some LUTs can crush shadows or blow highlights. Make sure the one you pick suits your footage.

You do not need LUTs at all if you prefer a fully manual approach. They are just tools to speed up certain looks.

---

## 7. Handling Different Scenes with Unique Looks

Sometimes, you want specific sequences to have a distinct color style. For instance, flashbacks might be slightly desaturated or tinted in sepia, or dream scenes might have a milky glow. If you do this, confirm that the transitions between scenes still make sense:

1. **Visual Cues:** If you jump from a normal look to a stylized look, the audience can tell it is a different kind of moment (like a memory).
2. **Stay Consistent Inside Each Sequence:** Do not switch color styles within the same scene unless the script calls for it (such as lights flickering).
3. **Communicate with the Team:** Make sure the director and editor (if different from you) know which scenes have special grading.

This method can strengthen storytelling by clearly marking changes in time, mood, or reality.

# 8. Overview of Visual Effects (VFX)

Visual effects can range from simple tasks like removing wires or background objects to adding whole 3D environments. For many independent projects, typical effects might include:

- **Green Screen Composites:** Replacing a green background with a new location.
- **Sky Replacements:** Swapping a dull sky for a more dramatic one.
- **Object Removal:** Painting out unwanted items like boom mics or signage.
- **Screen Replacements:** Putting the correct image on a TV or phone screen that was blank during filming.

Complex CGI or motion capture is beyond the scope of many small crews, but you can still do basic compositing with modern software. The key is to plan well so your shots are easy to manipulate.

---

# 9. Planning Effects During Production

If you know you will add an effect in post, plan it on set:

1. **Green or Blue Screen:** If filming an actor against a background you intend to replace, light the screen evenly and separate the actor from it so you do not get color spill.
2. **Tracking Markers:** If you want to track a camera move for a sky replacement or 3D element, place small markers in the scene that software can follow.
3. **Minimal Motion Blur:** Excessive blur can complicate keying or object removal. Keep your shutter speed appropriate.
4. **Reference Shots:** Sometimes, filming a clean plate (no actors) helps you remove elements or layer things later.

A bit of preparation can save hours in post. Also, keep in mind that simpler is often better for smaller teams without big budgets.

---

## 10. Basic Green Screen Techniques

When you have a shot with a green background:

1. **Keying:** In your software (like After Effects, DaVinci Resolve Fusion, or a plug-in in Premiere Pro), use a keyer effect. You pick the green color range to remove, leaving the subject.
2. **Spill Suppression:** Green light can reflect onto the subject's edges. Use a spill suppressor to reduce that green fringe.
3. **Lighting Match:** The background you place behind the subject should match the lighting direction and intensity on the subject. If the subject is lit from the left, but your background has sunlight from the right, it looks fake.
4. **Add a Subtle Blur or Grain:** Sometimes, blending is improved by applying a small blur or matching film grain so the subject does not pop out unnaturally.

Green screen can look seamless or can look bad depending on how carefully you film and key it. Practice is vital.

---

## 11. Object Removal and Clean-Up

Maybe you have a microphone in the top corner or a sign you could not move during filming. You can remove it with digital methods:

1. **Masking and Cloning:** If the background is simple (like a clear sky), you might duplicate adjacent pixels to cover the unwanted object.
2. **Tracking:** If the camera moves, you can track the motion so the cloned patch moves correctly in sync.
3. **Content-Aware Fill (Some Software):** Tools like After Effects have content-aware fill to guess what the background would be. This works best on predictable textures.
4. **Keep It Short:** If the unwanted element is visible for only a moment, you might need fewer frames to fix.

Time and patience are key. Even small fixes can require frame-by-frame work if the shot is complicated.

## 12. Adding Simple Effects: Muzzle Flashes, Fire, or Light Rays

You can find stock footage or plug-ins for effects like muzzle flashes for gunfire, sparks, or atmospheric elements. The basic process is:

1. **Place the Effect as an Overlay:** Set the blend mode to something like "Add" or "Screen" so the black background disappears.
2. **Match Movement:** If the gun recoils, keyframe your effect to line up with the gun barrel.
3. **Light Interaction:** For a muzzle flash, briefly brighten the actor's face or the nearby walls. That sells the flash as real.
4. **Sound Sync:** Do not forget the correct sound effect. Visual alone is not enough.

Small touches like adding a slight glow on surrounding objects can raise the realism of these simple effects.

---

## 13. Motion Tracking Basics

**Motion tracking** follows a point or pattern in the footage so you can attach something to that movement. For example, you might replace a sign on a moving car or track text to a building's side:

1. **Choose a Good Track Point:** Look for an area of high contrast that remains visible through the shot.
2. **Run the Tracker:** Your software will analyze frames and produce track data.
3. **Apply Data to an Element:** Your replacement image or text moves in sync with the track.
4. **Refine:** Sometimes the tracker slips. You can correct by adjusting the track or adding keyframes.

Motion tracking can fix wobbly composites or anchor effects to real-world items. It can also add moving text or creative overlays to a scene.

## 14. CGI or 3D Elements at a Basic Level

If you want to add a simple 3D model, the steps might include:

1. **Model/Asset:** You get or create a 3D model, perhaps from an online library.
2. **Matchmove (Camera Tracking):** If the camera moves in 3D space, you track it so the software knows how the camera is oriented.
3. **Render the 3D Object:** You place it in the scene with a 3D program. You match lighting and color so it looks natural.
4. **Composite:** In your compositing tool, you layer the rendered frames with your live-action plate. Add shadows, reflections, or color adjustments to blend.

This can become complex quickly, which is why many smaller productions keep CGI minimal. But it is still an option for certain shots if you plan carefully and have basic 3D knowledge or a collaborator who does.

---

## 15. Working with a Dedicated VFX Artist

Just as with color or sound, you might bring in a specialist:

1. **Explain the Shot:** Provide the raw footage, any references, and a clear idea of what you want changed or added.
2. **Ensure They Have the Needed Data:** This might mean camera settings, lens info, or a clean plate.
3. **Review Drafts:** The VFX artist sends versions. You provide feedback.
4. **Integrate into Edit:** Once final, place it in your timeline. Check color consistency.
5. **Budget and Time:** Good VFX can be time-consuming. Prepare for multiple revisions if the effect is complex.

Hiring a skilled person can free you to focus on other tasks, but you must communicate your vision to avoid misunderstandings.

## 16. Checking the Final Look with Color and VFX

When your color work and effects are done, watch the film from start to finish:

- **Shot Consistency:** If you have a big color shift, does it feel odd between scenes?
- **VFX Realism:** Does the effect call too much attention to itself? Sometimes a subtle approach is better.
- **Skin Tones:** Even with a stylized grade, keep human skin looking plausible unless you want a fantasy effect.
- **Lighting Continuity:** Check if any added elements or backgrounds match the light in the original footage.

Remember, the best results are often those that go unnoticed by the average viewer.

---

## 17. Rendering and Performance Issues

High-resolution footage plus color effects and VFX can bog down your computer. Some tips:

1. **Proxy Files for VFX:** Use smaller proxies if the software supports them, then switch to full-res for final rendering.
2. **Pre-Render Complex Shots:** In some software, you can render heavy effect shots into a single video file and replace the original to ease playback.
3. **Hardware Upgrades:** A powerful GPU can speed up color grading and compositing.
4. **Patience with Renders:** Complex composites or 4K timelines can take hours to render. Plan your schedule accordingly.

Check your final render carefully. Sometimes artifacts or glitches appear that were not visible in real-time previews.

## 18. Brief Notes on HDR (High Dynamic Range)

HDR is a technology that displays a wider range of brightness and color. If you plan for HDR:

- **HDR Workflow:** You need an HDR monitor, HDR-capable software, and possibly special color grading steps.
- **Output Requirements:** Platforms like Netflix or certain theaters might require HDR deliverables.
- **Extra Care:** Grading for HDR is more complex because you can push brightness far beyond standard range.
- **Fallback Versions:** You often need a standard version too, because not everyone has HDR screens.

For most smaller projects, standard dynamic range (SDR) is sufficient, but HDR is growing in popularity.

---

## 19. Managing Multiple Color Versions

Sometimes you need a different color version for a producer's request or for marketing:

1. **Save Projects with Names or Versions:** For example, "Project_Graded_v1," "Project_Graded_v2_warmer," etc.
2. **Export Reference Stills:** If you are trying two different looks, share screenshots or a short sample video with the team.
3. **Consistent Approach to Scenes:** If you do a radical change, ensure you apply it consistently across related scenes.
4. **Backup Original Project Files:** In case you want to revert to an earlier grade.

Avoid confusion by labeling carefully. If you mix them, you might end up with mismatched shots in the same film.

---

## 20. Quality Check on Many Devices

As with sound, color and VFX can appear different on various screens:

1. **Check on Computer Monitor and TV:** The dynamic range and color might vary.
2. **Smartphone Preview:** Many people watch content on phones. Ensure your grading does not crush details on small displays.
3. **Avoid Overly Dark Scenes:** Some might look okay on a bright reference monitor, but become nearly unwatchable in average or bright rooms.
4. **Any Color Shifts?:** If your calibration is not standard, your carefully graded scene might look too green or too red on normal TVs. You might do a final pass to ensure a middle-ground look.

If possible, watch your near-final version in a setting similar to your audience's environment. Catch issues before they do.

---

## 21. Minor vs. Major VFX: Knowing Your Limits

Your story might only need a few small fixes, or you might have an ambitious approach with big VFX sequences:

- **Minor Tweaks:** Quick wire removals, subtle sky replacements, or adding a digital sign. These are common in many films.
- **Major Shots:** If your script calls for creatures, big environment expansions, or explosions, be sure you have either a large budget or a skilled team.
- **Time Factor:** Complex VFX can add months to your post-production. Plan accordingly.
- **Test Early:** If you rely heavily on VFX, do test shots well before the final shoot so you know it is possible to achieve the desired results.

Realistic expectations help you avoid half-finished effects or poorly integrated CGI that hurts your movie.

---

## 22. Keeping the Story in Focus

With color and VFX, it is easy to get carried away. Always ask: does this reinforce the story? Some advanced color or flashy effects might look "cool," but distract from the plot or performances. For example, if you push an extreme teal-orange grade on a tender love scene, you might overshadow the gentle mood. Or if you add random lens flares and spark effects for no reason, viewers might wonder why. Let the script and tone guide your choices. The best color and VFX are those that help the audience connect more deeply with the film.

## 23. Collaboration with the Director of Photography (DP)

If you are not the DP, show them your color progress. They spent time designing lighting on set, so they might have a vision for how shots should look:

1. **Reference Images or LUTs:** The DP may have recommended a LUT on set for a certain style. Honor that if it suits the final direction.
2. **Ask for Input on Key Scenes:** If you are making major color changes, confirm it does not clash with the DP's plan.
3. **Discuss Any Conflicts:** If you think a scene needs more contrast but the DP disagrees, talk it through. A middle ground might be best.

A film benefits when the DP's original lighting choices and your color process align. You do not want to undo their lighting by drastically changing everything in post without reason.

## 24. Final Rendering for Distribution

When you are satisfied with your color and VFX, you will export the final version:

1. **Set Proper Output Settings:** Match your distribution plan (e.g., 1080p or 4K). Use a good codec for high quality (like ProRes or DNxHD) for the master copy.
2. **Check Frame Rate:** Keep it consistent with your original project (e.g., 24fps).
3. **Preserve Color Space:** If you used a log workflow, ensure your final export is in the correct space (Rec.709 or otherwise).
4. **Watch the Final Export:** Sometimes compression artifacts or color shifts can appear. Doing a quick run-through is essential.

Keep a master export in very high quality. Then you can make smaller or more compressed copies for the web, festivals, or general sharing.

## 25. Chapter 17 Key Points Recap

- **Color Correction** fixes exposure and white balance issues so all shots look consistent. **Color Grading** then adds a style that fits the story's mood.
- You can use built-in editing software tools or specialized programs like DaVinci Resolve. Scopes (waveform, vectorscope, histogram) give objective guidance.
- **VFX** can be simple (object removal, sky replacement) or more advanced (green screen, CGI elements). Plan for them during production to reduce post headaches.
- For green screen, lighting and distance from the backdrop are vital to avoid ugly color spill.
- Matching lighting and color in composited shots helps them blend. Subtle details like shadows and slight color tints can make or break realism.
- Keep the story in mind. Do not let color or flashy effects distract from character moments or plot points.
- Collaborate with your DP or a VFX artist when possible. Good communication ensures you respect the original vision and get professional results.
- Test your final color and effects on different screens. Render in high quality and keep backups.
- Balanced, polished color and well-integrated VFX can enhance your film's overall impact without taking attention away from the heart of the story.

By mastering these color and visual effects steps, you boost your film's visual appeal. Next, in **Chapter 18**, we will look at **Planning Your Film's Release**. You will learn how to take your finished movie and share it with the world—be it through streaming, festivals, or local showings. Having a plan for release ensures all your hard work reaches the widest audience possible.

# CHAPTER 18: PLANNING YOUR FILM'S RELEASE

You have spent a long time writing, shooting, and polishing your movie. Now it is time to think about sharing it with viewers. A film release can take many routes—online platforms, local theaters, film festivals, or direct distribution deals. Each path has pros and cons, and no single plan works for everyone. In this chapter, we will explore how to make a release strategy, from setting goals and picking the right platforms to handling publicity and dealing with the required marketing materials. By the end, you will have a clearer picture of how to ensure your movie gets the attention it deserves.

## 1. Defining Your Film's Goals

Before you pick a release method, ask yourself: *What do I want from this film?* Some common goals include:

1. **Artistic Recognition:** You might want to build a reputation as a filmmaker, gain festival awards, or gather critical acclaim.
2. **Profit or Return on Investment:** If investors financed your movie, you likely need to find a way to recoup costs and possibly earn profits.
3. **Public Awareness of a Topic:** Some films aim to highlight a social cause or push for awareness.
4. **Portfolio Showcase:** For students or first-time directors, releasing a film might be about showing skills to get future gigs.

Your main goal shapes your release plan. For instance, if you want festival acclaim, you might focus on the festival circuit first. If you want quick online exposure, you might skip festivals and go straight to a streaming platform.

## 2. Considering Different Release Paths

Several major channels exist to share your film:

1. **Film Festivals:** Great for exposure, networking, and possibly winning awards. But the selection process can be competitive, and festivals usually require an entry fee.

2. **Theatrical Release:** Traditional, but tough for indie films without distribution partners. Local theaters or small arthouses might screen your movie for a limited run.
3. **Online Platforms:** Options range from YouTube or Vimeo for free, to paid platforms like Amazon Prime Video, iTunes, or niche streaming services.
4. **Self-Distribution:** You can host the film on your own site and charge for downloads. This requires marketing to get people to buy it.
5. **TV or Cable Sales:** Some networks buy indie content, but it often requires a sales agent or aggregator.

Evaluate each path. Festivals offer prestige, but you might wait months for decisions and your film might not get accepted. Online is quick to publish but requires a solid marketing push to stand out among millions of videos. Theatrical releases are costly and rarely recoup costs for small projects without an existing fan base.

---

## 3. Building Early Buzz

While still in post-production, you can begin building awareness:

1. **Social Media Updates:** Share behind-the-scenes photos, short teasers, or progress updates on platforms like Instagram, Twitter, or Facebook.
2. **Production Blog or Newsletter:** Some filmmakers run a small blog or mailing list to keep interested people informed.
3. **Engage Local Press:** If your film is tied to a local community or subject, local newspapers or radio might do a small piece about it.
4. **Teaser Posters:** Even a simple poster or concept art helps potential viewers remember your project.

Early buzz does not have to be huge. The goal is to spark curiosity so that when you officially release, a core group is ready to watch or support you.

---

## 4. Creating a Trailer

A trailer is one of the best marketing tools. Keep it concise and interesting:

1. **Length:** Usually 1-2 minutes is enough. Shorter teasers (30-60 seconds) can also work well online.
2. **Show the Hook:** If your film is about an unusual topic or has a strong emotional core, highlight that in the first few seconds.
3. **Avoid Spoilers:** Tease, do not give away key twists.
4. **Visual and Audio Impact:** Good music, sharp editing, and a sense of pacing matter as much as the content.
5. **Clear Info:** End with the film title, release date (if set), or "Coming Soon." If you are driving traffic to a website or social media, put that link or handle.

Update or refine the trailer if your release plan changes. A polished trailer can also help with festival submissions, as some festivals watch them to get a feel for the movie.

---

## 5. Festival Strategy

Film festivals can increase your film's credibility:

1. **Research Tiers of Festivals:** Some events are highly prestigious (like Cannes, Sundance, Toronto), but extremely competitive. Many smaller or regional festivals can still offer great exposure and awards.
2. **Submission Deadlines and Fees:** Check early, regular, and late deadlines. Late fees can be high. Plan your budget for submission fees.
3. **Premiere Status:** Some top festivals want a world or regional premiere, so if you show it publicly first, you might lose eligibility.
4. **Screening Formats:** Many require DCP (Digital Cinema Package) or a certain type of file. Ensure you can provide it.
5. **Networking:** If accepted, attend the festival if possible. Meeting other filmmakers, distributors, or journalists can open doors for future projects.

Not all films benefit from festivals. It depends on your genre and target audience. However, a well-chosen festival run can lead to press coverage and distribution interest.

---

## 6. Approaching Distributors or Sales Agents

If you aim for a wider release:

1. **Distributors:** They handle marketing and distribution, sometimes paying you an advance or sharing revenue. They might place your film in theaters or on streaming platforms.
2. **Sales Agents:** They shop your movie to different territories or platforms, taking a commission.
3. **When to Approach:** Usually after you have a finished film or a strong screener.
4. **Look for a Good Match:** Some distributors focus on horror, others on documentaries. Pick one that suits your genre.
5. **Contracts:** Read carefully. Some deals might tie up your rights for many years with minimal returns. Seek legal advice if you can.

Many indie directors do not land a major distributor. A smaller or niche partner might still help reach a specific audience. Keep realistic expectations.

---

## 7. Self-Distribution Options

If you cannot find or do not want a distributor, you can self-distribute:

1. **Video on Demand (VOD) Platforms:** Amazon Prime Video Direct, Vimeo On Demand, Gumroad, or even your own site can let people rent or buy.
2. **YouTube or Ad-Based Platforms:** You might earn revenue from ads if you get enough views.
3. **Direct Sales:** Selling DVDs or Blu-rays at local events, or from your website, can still work if your audience prefers physical media.
4. **Merchandise:** T-shirts, posters, or soundtrack albums might bring some extra income.
5. **Promotional Efforts:** With self-distribution, marketing is on you. You must handle social media, press outreach, and possibly pay for ads if you want bigger reach.

You keep control and do not share profits with a distributor, but the workload can be high, and success depends on how well you promote the film.

## 8. Timing Your Release

Picking the right release date or window matters:

1. **Avoid Big Competition:** If you release online the same day as a major blockbuster on streaming, you might be overshadowed.
2. **Seasonal Themes:** If your film is holiday-themed, aim for the relevant season. If it is about education, maybe tie it to back-to-school months.
3. **Sync with Festivals:** If you plan to premiere at a festival, do not release it publicly before the festival screening (some festivals have rules about that).
4. **Build Anticipation:** If possible, set a date a few weeks or months ahead. Use that time to market.

Do not overthink it, but do not rush out your film the moment it is done. A bit of planning can help you hit a quieter period where your film stands out.

---

## 9. Press Kits and Marketing Materials

To attract media coverage or festival attention, prepare a **press kit**:

1. **Synopsis:** A short summary of your film's story and main theme.
2. **Cast and Crew Bios:** Key people involved, plus any notable achievements.
3. **Production Stills:** High-quality stills from the movie or behind the scenes.
4. **Director's Statement:** Why did you make this film? What is the message or inspiration?
5. **Trailer and Clips:** Easy links or files for journalists to watch.
6. **Contact Info:** For interviews or more details.

A press kit can be a simple PDF or a page on your site. Make it easy for bloggers, journalists, or festival staff to find crucial info.

---

## 10. Social Media Strategy

Even if you do not have a giant marketing budget, social media can amplify your presence:

1. **Pick Key Platforms:** You do not have to be on every platform. Focus on where your likely audience hangs out.
2. **Regular Posting:** Share production trivia, quotes from the film, short clips, or behind-the-scenes photos.
3. **Hashtags and Collaboration:** Use relevant hashtags. Tag cast or crew. If an actor has a following, coordinate posts.
4. **Contests or Teasers:** You can run small contests for free screening links or signed posters.
5. **Engage with Fans:** Answer questions, thank people for sharing, build a sense of connection.

Avoid spamming or random posts. Consistency and genuine interaction can build a loyal following who will watch your movie once it is out.

## 11. Local Screenings and Community Events

Showing your film locally can be a big morale boost and can lead to press coverage:

1. **Community Centers or Colleges:** They might rent a small auditorium.
2. **Small Theaters or Arthouse Cinemas:** Some let indie filmmakers rent the space for a premiere night.
3. **Q&A Sessions:** After the screening, you or key cast members can answer questions. This personal touch often excites viewers and might encourage local media to cover the event.
4. **Ticket Sales or Donations:** You can charge a modest fee or ask for donations.

Local screenings can also serve as a test-run to see audience reactions before a wider release.

## 12. Working with Online Influencers

Influencers on YouTube, TikTok, or Instagram might help promote your film:

1. **Identify Relevant Influencers:** If your film is about cooking, find food influencers. If it is sci-fi, find sci-fi reviewers.

2. **Send a Screener:** A private link so they can watch. Ask if they would share their thoughts.
3. **Short Interviews or Collabs:** Some might invite you to talk about the film on their channel.
4. **Be Respectful:** They get many requests. Personalize your message, show you know their content.

This path works if your film has a niche angle that connects with a certain influencer's audience.

## 13. Handling Distribution Platforms

Each online platform has its own rules:

1. **Amazon Prime Video Direct:** You upload your film, set a price (if you want to rent or sell), or make it free for Prime members with a revenue per hour watched. The interface can be tricky, and Amazon can remove your film if it does not meet their technical or content standards.
2. **Vimeo On Demand:** You control the price, keep a large share of revenue, but you must drive traffic there.
3. **YouTube Movies:** More for big studios, but you can also offer your film as a paid view. Or you could upload it free with ads if you want maximum exposure.
4. **Niche Platforms:** Horror films might do well on specialized horror streaming sites, or documentaries might find a home on certain doc-focused services.
5. **Aggregators:** Services that submit your film to iTunes, Google Play, or other stores for a fee or revenue share.

Check each platform's compression guidelines, artwork requirements, and revenue model. Summaries or descriptions must be punchy and professional. You might need closed captions or subtitles to comply with certain rules.

## 14. Pricing and Monetization Tips

If you want viewers to pay:

1. **Compare Market Rates:** Look at similar indie films. Typically, a rental might cost a few dollars, a purchase a bit more.
2. **Discount Periods:** Consider an early-bird price or a short free window to build reviews.
3. **Bundle Extras:** Add behind-the-scenes videos or extended interviews to sweeten the deal.
4. **Global Availability:** If you open to worldwide markets, do you have subtitle options or regional pricing?

Balancing a fair price with encouraging people to watch can be tricky. Some prefer wide exposure at a lower price or even free, hoping to gain fans for future projects.

## 15. Getting Reviews and Ratings

Positive reviews help discoverability:

1. **Film Review Websites and Blogs:** Reach out to critics or niche bloggers who cover your genre.
2. **Rotten Tomatoes or IMDb Ratings:** Encourage viewers to leave ratings if they liked the film.
3. **Press Screeners:** A private link you share with reviewers or journalists.
4. **Be Polite with Criticism:** Not all reviews will be glowing. Thank reviewers anyway and focus on the constructive points.

Even a few good quotes from credible sources can boost your film's credibility in marketing materials.

## 16. Handling an Online Premiere

If you do a scheduled online premiere:

1. **Set a Time and Date:** Promote it like an event. People can watch simultaneously, maybe with a live chat.
2. **Build Hype:** Post countdowns, last-minute teasers.
3. **Post-Screening Q&A:** Maybe do a live stream after for viewer questions.

4. **Replay Options:** Decide if the film stays online for free after the premiere or if you switch to a paywall or remove it altogether.

A coordinated online premiere can create a sense of urgency and excitement, especially if you or the cast interacts in real time.

## 17. Merchandise and Crowdfunding Follow-Up

If you used crowdfunding to finance the film:

1. **Fulfill Rewards:** Send digital downloads or physical items to backers. They helped make the film happen, so treat them well.
2. **Merch Store:** If fans want T-shirts, posters, or special edition DVDs, set up a simple online store.
3. **Community Building:** Keep those backers in the loop about the film's progress, festival showings, or future projects.
4. **Updates on Income:** Some crowdfunders like to see how the film did financially, though you are not required to share all details.

Turning supporters into long-term fans can help your next project.

## 18. Handling Piracy and Legal Notes

Sadly, piracy happens. But there are steps:

1. **Content ID or Takedown Notices:** If you find illegal uploads, you can request platforms remove them.
2. **Watermarks or Soft Security:** Some filmmakers place subtle watermarks on screeners or release only low-quality files for public previews.
3. **Accept Some Risk:** Unless you have a big legal budget, you might not stop all piracy. Focus on building your official release presence so legit viewers can easily find it.
4. **Contracts:** If you are distributing via a partnership, read how they handle anti-piracy measures.

While piracy is frustrating, many viewers prefer safe, official ways to watch if they are available and affordable.

## 19. Tracking Your Success

After release, track how the film performs:

1. **Analytics on Platforms:** If on Amazon, you see rentals or purchases. Vimeo might show you views and revenue. YouTube shows watch time and demographics.
2. **Social Media Mentions:** Track comments, shares, or hashtags to gauge audience feedback.
3. **Reviews and Ratings:** IMDb or letterboxd can show how viewers rate the film.
4. **Email List or Followers:** If you keep track of your mailing list growth or social following, it can show if your film is attracting more interest.

Use this info to see what worked or did not. Did certain promotions spike views? Did a festival mention help? These lessons guide future projects.

## 20. Staying Realistic About Earnings

Many indie films do not make large sums:

- **Breaking Even is Commonly the First Goal:** If you can earn back your production costs, that is a success in the indie world.
- **Small But Steady Income:** Over time, sales or streaming royalties might trickle in, especially if your film finds a niche audience.
- **Building a Catalog:** Some filmmakers produce multiple small films, each adding a bit of revenue.
- **Focus on Career Steps:** Even if one film does not earn a lot, it can lead to more opportunities or build your reputation.

Approach the release with a balanced view. If you market well, you can find your audience, but do not expect instant riches unless you have a rare breakout hit.

## 21. Future Projects and Lifespan

Your film can keep living:

1. **Catalogue Over Time:** Some older films experience renewed interest if an actor later becomes famous or if the topic becomes relevant.
2. **Follow-Up or Sequels:** If you built a fan base, you might do a related film.
3. **TV or Educational Licenses:** Documentaries or socially focused films can be licensed for classrooms, libraries, or TV segments.
4. **Public Screenings Years Later:** You might still get invited to local film nights or genre events.

Keeping your film's files organized means you can re-render new versions (like 4K or different language subtitles) if the need arises.

## 22. Working with a Publicist or PR Agent

If you have funds, hiring a publicist helps:

1. **Press Releases:** They craft professional statements and send them to media outlets.
2. **Media Contacts:** They might already know journalists or editors who cover films.
3. **Interview Scheduling:** They can arrange interviews for you or your cast.
4. **Timing of Publicity:** They plan the best times to release announcements so you get the most coverage.

This can be expensive, so weigh the cost versus potential reach. Sometimes, for small films, direct outreach is sufficient, but a pro can open bigger doors.

## 23. Collaborations and Cross-Promotions

You can team up with others:

1. **Similar Films:** Maybe run a double feature online or do a watch party with another indie director.
2. **Topic-Based Groups:** If your film is about a historic event, partner with a museum or a local history club.

3. **Local Businesses:** If your movie's setting involves coffee shops or a certain brand, they might be interested in cross-promotion.
4. **Charity Connections:** For documentary or socially minded films, a charity might host a screening to raise funds, giving you both publicity and an audience.

Partnerships can expand your reach and tap into existing communities who will enjoy your content.

## 24. Final Release Checklist

Before you go live:

- **Final Master File:** Make sure it is the best version of your film—color graded, with the final sound mix, and correct aspect ratio.
- **Subtitles or Captions:** Many platforms require them. They also help reach viewers who are deaf or speak different languages.
- **Poster and Key Art:** Eye-catching artwork to use as a thumbnail or ad.
- **Trailer Online:** Ready to share on social and in press kits.
- **Official Release Date:** Announce it so your followers know when and where to watch.
- **Backups:** Store your film's master files and project data on multiple drives or cloud storage.

Tick these boxes to avoid last-minute scrambles or missing details.

## 25. Chapter 18 Key Points Recap

- Define your goals—artistic recognition, profit, awareness, or personal portfolio building. This guides your release plan.
- You can focus on festivals, theatrical (though challenging), online streaming platforms, or self-distribution. Each route has pros and cons.
- Build awareness early with social media posts, a solid trailer, and a press kit.
- If going for festivals, watch out for deadlines, premiere rules, and necessary screening formats.

- For broader distribution, consider approaching distributors or sales agents but read contracts carefully.
- Self-distribution requires strong marketing. Online platforms vary in revenue models and submission steps.
- Time your release and plan promotional efforts with care. A well-crafted trailer, local screenings, or influencer partnerships can help.
- Keep your release schedule realistic. Breaking even is often success in the indie film space.
- Always track performance, gather reviews, and adapt. Your film can find new audiences over time, especially if you remain active in promoting it.

With a thorough release plan, your film stands a better chance of reaching viewers and making a mark. In the next chapter, **Chapter 19**, we will talk about **Film Festivals and Networking** in more detail, focusing on how to approach festivals effectively and build connections that help your career. Even if you already touched on festivals here, we will go deeper into the logistics, do's, and don'ts of the festival world, plus how to make the most of networking events and film markets.

# CHAPTER 19: FILM FESTIVALS AND NETWORKING

Making a film is one part of the process. Once you have a completed movie, you have to get it seen. Film festivals can be great spots for gathering interest, winning awards, and meeting people who can help your future projects. Networking is also important. This does not mean just handing out business cards; it means building real connections with folks who share your passion or can offer you opportunities. In this chapter, we will look at how film festivals work, tips for entering them, and how to expand your circle in an honest, practical way. By the end, you should know how to make the best of the festival scene and other networking chances so your film (and your career) can move forward.

## 1. Why Film Festivals Matter

Film festivals are special events where people watch and talk about movies. They often include:

1. **Screenings:** Your film might be shown to a live audience on a big screen.
2. **Awards:** Some festivals hand out prizes, which can boost your film's status.
3. **Industry Panels:** Experts speak about trends or share advice.
4. **Social Events:** Parties, mixers, or question-and-answer sessions where you can meet other filmmakers.

Festivals help in different ways:

- **Audience Feedback:** Watching your film with a live crowd tells you a lot about how they respond.
- **Press Coverage:** Some festivals have media presence, leading to reviews or interviews.
- **Distribution Doors:** Distributors or sales agents often attend, scouting for interesting projects.
- **Long-Term Contacts:** People you meet might become partners, collaborators, or friends for future work.

Not all films benefit from festivals, but if you aim for recognition or want to see how your film stacks up, it can be a solid choice.

## 2. Types of Film Festivals

There are thousands of festivals worldwide. They vary in size, focus, and prestige. Some broad categories:

1. **Top-Tier Festivals:** Events like Cannes, Venice, Berlin, Sundance, Toronto. These are famous and hard to get into. They tend to look for world or international premieres.
2. **Mid-Level or Regional Festivals:** Examples include many city-specific events (like Seattle, Austin, or Chicago). They still have decent industry presence but are more accessible.
3. **Niche or Genre Festivals:** Focused on horror, documentary, short films, or animation. If your film fits a category, you might find a loyal audience there.
4. **Student or Smaller Local Festivals:** Perfect for new filmmakers or smaller projects. They have fewer submissions and can be more welcoming.

Before picking festivals, think about your film's style and subject. For example, if it is a sci-fi short, a sci-fi festival might be ideal. If it is a serious drama, a big general festival might be better.

## 3. Submitting to Festivals: Process and Tips

1. **Choose Wisely:** Each submission can cost money (entry fee). Avoid sending your film to every event on Earth. Focus on events that match your film's style or your goals.
2. **Mind the Deadlines:** Festivals have early, regular, and late deadlines. Early deadlines are cheaper. Late ones can be quite expensive.
3. **Check Premiere Rules:** Some top-tier festivals want world premieres. If you have already shown the film publicly (even online), you might disqualify yourself from certain events.
4. **Submission Platforms:** Many festivals use websites like FilmFreeway or Withoutabox (though Withoutabox closed in 2019, so FilmFreeway is now

the main one). They let you upload your film and details once, then submit to multiple events.
5. **Polished Screener:** Your film should be in final form (good color, sound, subtitles if needed). Some festivals let you send a rough cut, but that can be risky if the final version differs a lot.
6. **Fees and Waivers:** If the fee is high, see if you qualify for a waiver (for students, for example). But do not rely on waivers for everything.

Try not to be discouraged by rejections. Many festivals receive thousands of entries for a limited number of slots. Keep track of each festival's response dates so you are not left guessing.

---

## 4. Festival Preparations: Materials and Mindset

If a festival accepts your film:

1. **DCP or Other Format:** Some theaters require a Digital Cinema Package. You may need to pay a professional service to create this if you cannot do it yourself. Smaller festivals might accept a Blu-ray or a digital file.
2. **Promotional Items:** Posters, postcards, or flyers can help promote your screening around the festival venue.
3. **Press Kit:** Have a short synopsis, cast/crew bios, and high-quality stills. The festival might put this on their website or share it with local media.
4. **Subtitles or Captions:** If the festival is international or your film is in a language that is not the event's main language, you need subtitles.
5. **Travel Plans:** Decide if you can attend in person. Some festivals offer help (housing or travel deals), but many do not. Budget accordingly if you want to be there.

Take advantage of your screening slot. Show up early, watch how the tech team sets up, and confirm your film's audio and visuals look correct.

---

## 5. At the Festival: Screenings and Q&As

When the day comes and your film is shown:

- **Arrive Early:** Make sure the projection is correct. If there is a sound issue or color problem, talk to the festival staff.
- **Introduce Your Film:** Some festivals let you give a short intro. Keep it brief; do not spoil the plot.
- **Q&A Afterward:** Be ready for audience questions. They might ask about the story, filming process, or your future plans. Keep answers friendly and honest.
- **Collect Feedback:** Listeners might approach you after the screening. This is a great time to hear opinions or gather emails for your mailing list.
- **Thank the Staff:** Festivals run on dedicated workers. Show appreciation.

Some festivals also host awards ceremonies. If your film is nominated, celebrate the nomination. If you win, that can help in marketing. But if you do not, that is common—use the event for contacts and learning.

---

## 6. Networking Without Being Pushy

Networking is more than just handing out cards. It is about forming genuine bonds. Some pointers:

1. **Start Conversations:** Instead of leading with "Here's my card," ask them about their film, or what they like about the festival so far. Show genuine interest in others' work.
2. **Ask Simple Questions:** "How did you find the shoot?" or "What inspired your story?" This can open a friendly talk.
3. **Give Them Space:** If someone is busy or not in the mood, do not force it. You can always circle back later.
4. **Listen More Than You Talk:** People appreciate it when you pay attention rather than just pitching yourself.
5. **Know When to Share Info:** If they ask about your film or want to continue the conversation, that is your moment.
6. **Follow Up Politely:** If you get a business card or contact info, send a short, polite message later, like "Great meeting you at the festival—let's keep in touch."

Genuine networking is about mutual help. Maybe you can offer them insight or introduce them to someone else. Look for ways to be helpful, not just to get help.

## 7. Leveraging Social Events and Mixers

Festivals often have parties, mixers, or VIP receptions. They might feel awkward if you are shy, but they are key places to meet folks. A few tips:

1. **Go in a Group or with a Friend:** If you are not comfortable alone, bring a fellow filmmaker or friend. That can make it easier to talk to new people.
2. **Spot Common Ground:** People might wear badges that list their projects or roles. If you see someone is also an editor, say hello and discuss editing.
3. **Keep Conversations Natural:** It is not a job interview. Discuss favorite movies, experiences at the festival, or random normal life stuff. Later, you can mention your own film.
4. **Exchange Contacts If It Makes Sense:** Do not push it on everyone. But if someone is truly interested, a quick card or digital link is fine.
5. **Mind the Time:** Do not monopolize someone's entire evening. If it is going well, sure, but if they have to circulate, let them go politely.

---

## 8. Panel Discussions and Workshops

Many festivals host panels where experts talk about topics like distribution, screenwriting, or cinematography. Attend these sessions to:

1. **Learn from Pros:** They share insight you might not get elsewhere.
2. **Ask Smart Questions:** If they do a Q&A, a short question can get you noticed. Do not hog the mic.
3. **Meet Like-Minded People:** Others in the audience share your interests. You might start conversations afterward.
4. **Take Notes:** Jot down key advice or contact info for resources they mention.

Sometimes the panelists hang out after the talk. If you approach them politely and ask specific questions, it can lead to further contact.

---

## 9. Building an Ongoing Network

Networking does not end when the festival is over. Keep it alive:

1. **Connect Online:** Send a short message or friend request if it fits.
2. **Share Updates:** If you do a small screening in another city, mention it. People who liked your film might spread the word.
3. **Congratulate Others:** If you see someone you met has success (like an award or a new film), drop them a note saying "Congrats on your new project!"
4. **Collaborate If Opportunities Arise:** Maybe you can help with someone's short film as a DP or editor. This mutual support builds stronger ties.

A good network is about real relationships built over time, not quick transactions. Remember people's names, the subjects of their films, and be a supportive colleague. This often leads to unexpected doors opening later.

## 10. Expanding Beyond Festivals: Film Markets and Industry Events

**Film markets** (like the American Film Market, the European Film Market, or the Marché du Film at Cannes) are more about business deals:

- **Buyers, Sellers, Distributors:** They come to find content or strike deals.
- **Project Pitches:** Sometimes you can pitch your script or film idea if you have good materials.
- **Screenings for Buyers:** Some markets let you pay for a special screening to attract potential distributors.
- **High Competition:** Many people attend with big ambitions. You must stand out with a clear pitch and marketing.

These markets can be overwhelming if you are new. Sometimes it helps to have a sales agent or producer who knows how these events work. But it is still possible to attend, learn, and meet people on your own if you prepare thoroughly.

## 11. Online Networking for Filmmakers

Not every networking event is face-to-face. You can connect online:

1. **Filmmaker Forums and Groups:** Websites like Stage 32, various Facebook groups, or subreddits for indie film. You can share tips or seek advice.

2. **LinkedIn:** Some film professionals are active there. Keep your profile updated, join film groups, and post about your projects.
3. **Webinars and Virtual Events:** The past few years have seen more online panels or film gatherings. That can be a chance to learn or meet people from around the world.
4. **Email Introductions:** If you see someone's short on YouTube you admire, you can sometimes find their contact info and send a brief, thoughtful message.

Be respectful. Online spaces can turn toxic if people only self-promote. Contribute helpful info and be friendly. Over time, people trust you and might want to help out.

---

## 12. Press and Media Outreach

When your film gets into a festival or is about to release online, send a press release or info to:

1. **Local Outlets:** Community papers or TV stations often like stories about local residents' successes.
2. **Niche Blogs:** If your film is about a specific theme, a blog focusing on that topic might do a piece on it.
3. **Industry Websites:** Some film news sites or blogs highlight indie releases or festival picks.
4. **Building Good Relationships:** Journalists appreciate a clear, concise pitch. Provide a link to your trailer, a few stills, and a short summary.

Be polite, not pushy. If they do not respond, move on. They might be swamped or not see your film as a match. Any coverage you do get can be shared on your own site or social media for more credibility.

---

## 13. Handling Negative Feedback or Reviews

It happens to all filmmakers. Some people will not like your movie. If you see a bad review or harsh comment:

1. **Stay Calm:** Do not engage in a public fight.

2. **Consider If There's a Lesson:** Sometimes negative feedback highlights real issues you could learn from.
3. **Focus on the Positive:** Balance the negative with any good reviews or fan messages you have.
4. **Remember It's Subjective:** No film pleases everyone. The important thing is to keep improving.

Respectful replies to critics can show professionalism, but do not get dragged into arguments. If a comment is purely insulting or trolling, ignore it and move on.

## 14. Volunteer or Participate Behind the Scenes

If you cannot get your film into a certain festival or if you want more inside knowledge, consider volunteering:

1. **Working for a Festival:** You see how events run, meet the staff, and might connect with filmmakers.
2. **Helping Another Filmmaker:** If a peer's film is showing, offer your help. Maybe they need someone to handle Q&A or organize a side event.
3. **Learning the Ropes:** By seeing the festival from another angle, you gain tips on what they look for and how to stand out next time.

Volunteering also shows you are supportive of the film community. People might remember and invite you to future opportunities.

## 15. Using Networking for Your Next Projects

Networking is not just about the current movie. If you plan more films:

- **Look for Future Collaborators:** You might find a composer at a festival panel or an editor who loves your style.
- **Keep Tabs on Emerging Technology:** People you meet can clue you in on new cameras, software, or distribution trends.
- **Co-Production Possibilities:** Some countries or regions have grants for co-productions. A festival contact from another country might lead to a joint project.

- **Mentors and Advice:** A more experienced producer you met might guide you when you write your next script or sign a deal.

Networking is an ongoing journey. Each festival or event adds more puzzle pieces that can help you in the long run.

---

## 16. Planning Your Festival Budget

Entering many festivals can get expensive. Some practical steps:

1. **Prioritize:** Identify maybe 5-10 key festivals that best match your film.
2. **Early Bird Deadlines:** Submitting early can save you big money compared to the late deadline.
3. **Watch Out for Hidden Costs:** If you are accepted, you might need to travel, create a DCP, or print posters.
4. **Find Sponsorship:** A local business or organization might help fund your festival tour if your film has a community angle.
5. **Crowdfunding for the Festival Run:** Some filmmakers launch a small campaign specifically to cover festival fees and travel.

Keep track of submissions in a spreadsheet. Note the cost, deadline, and response date. This prevents confusion and helps you stay organized.

---

## 17. Hosting Your Own Screening Outside of Festivals

If you do not get into the events you wanted or you want more control:

1. **Rent a Small Theater or Space:** Some indie cinemas or community centers rent out rooms.
2. **Invite Media and Local Groups:** This can act like your own "micro-festival" for just your film (and maybe other local shorts).
3. **Sell Tickets or Make It Free:** Charging a small ticket fee might recoup costs. Or a free screening can attract more folks.
4. **Offer a Q&A:** Make it feel like a festival event, with a mini red carpet or an after-party.
5. **Promote Widely:** Use social media, local press, and flyers in coffee shops to get the word out.

Though it will not have the prestige of a known festival, it can still create buzz and gather audience feedback.

## 18. Dealing with Rejection Letters

Most filmmakers get many more rejections than acceptances from festivals. It is normal:

- **Do Not Take It Personally:** Selection can depend on a festival's theme, schedule, or the judges' taste.
- **Focus on Encouraging Responses:** If a programmer gives feedback on why they did not select it, that is valuable.
- **Try Other Festivals:** There are many out there. A "no" from one is not a "no" from all.
- **Maybe Revise Your Cut?:** If the festival feedback suggests pacing issues or confusion, you might do a small re-edit. But be careful about constantly changing the film just for festival reviewers.

Remember, big successes in film often faced multiple rejections before landing a breakthrough festival acceptance.

## 19. Building a Long-Term Presence

The festival circuit is not just about one film. Over the years, if you keep returning with new projects, staff and programmers might recognize you. Some steps:

1. **Stay in Touch with Festival Organizers:** If you met them and they liked your attitude, they might watch your future films with interest.
2. **Offer Your Help as a Speaker or Panelist:** If you become known for a certain skill, you can be invited to talk. That raises your profile.
3. **Social Media Interaction:** Follow festivals, comment on their posts, congratulate them on successful events. Show you are part of that community.
4. **Recommend Others' Films Too:** Festivals appreciate when filmmakers support each other. It reflects well on you if you champion quality films from peers.

As your reputation grows, you might find your next project gets more attention early in the submission process.

## 20. Common Festival and Networking Mistakes

1. **Being Aggressive About Promotion:** Constantly handing out flyers or pushing your business card at folks can annoy them.
2. **Taking Rejection As Personal:** It is not about you as a person. Programming is subjective.
3. **Forgetting Basic Info:** Some filmmakers cannot clearly explain their film's premise. Practice a short "elevator pitch."
4. **Ignoring Others:** If you only talk about your own film and never ask about theirs, you miss chances to bond.
5. **Not Following Up:** You collect cards, but never send a quick note later. That wastes potential connections.
6. **Skipping Thank-You Notes:** If someone helps you, always remember to thank them or mention them in your social posts.

## 21. Watching and Learning from Other Films

While at festivals, do not just stay for your screening:

1. **See Other Movies:** You discover new ideas, styles, or cinematic approaches.
2. **Analyze What Works:** Note how audiences react. Which comedic bits land well? Which dramatic parts create silence?
3. **Support Fellow Filmmakers:** They might return the favor by attending your screening.
4. **Meet Directors or Actors After Their Q&A:** Compliment them on specific things you enjoyed. This can spark further discussion.

Going to festivals is partly about learning from the films that made it in. This can help you spot trends or see how your next project could stand out.

## 22. Converting Festival Success into Distribution

If your film wins awards or generates excitement at a festival:

- **Press Releases:** Announce your win or positive response. Post it on your site, share on social media.
- **Reach Out to Distributors Again:** Mention the festival success. Sometimes a laurel from a known event opens doors.
- **Increase Online Views:** If your film is streaming, highlight those awards on the platform's thumbnail or description.
- **Invitations to Other Events:** Some festivals or smaller distributors keep an eye on winners from certain fests. They might invite your film or request to screen it.

Use that momentum, but do not rely on hype alone. Keep building your promotional efforts and be ready if new opportunities arrive.

---

## 23. Taking Advantage of Workshops and Labs

Some festivals have labs or development programs for scripts, works in progress, or new directors:

1. **Apply Early:** Spots can be limited. They might require a project sample or script.
2. **Intensive Learning:** They often bring mentors or industry pros to give feedback on your story or rough cut.
3. **Peer Support:** You will meet other filmmakers at the same stage. These ties can last years.
4. **Potential Funding or Grants:** Some labs include small grants or industry introductions that help you secure funds.

Labs and workshops can shape your craft and give you direct industry ties.

---

## 24. Be Open to Surprises

At festivals and networking events, not every connection is a planned transaction. You might meet a future friend at a random panel, or bump into a well-known director in the hallway. Some ways to be open:

- **Keep an Eye Out for Serendipity:** If someone mentions an idea that matches your project, ask to continue the conversation.
- **Attend Varied Events:** Do not just stick to your film's screening. Explore documentary blocks, short film blocks, etc.
- **Exchange Positive Energy:** People sense if you are open to genuine chat or just pushing your agenda.
- **Follow the Flow:** If a group invites you for coffee, go (if you can). You never know what might come from a casual talk.

---

## 25. Chapter 19 Key Points Recap

- Film festivals can be gateways to recognition, distribution, and valuable contacts.
- There are different tiers and types of festivals. Pick ones that fit your film's genre and goals.
- Prepare a strong submission, watch deadlines, and handle format requirements.
- At festivals, watch other screenings, network politely, and use Q&A sessions to meet fans and peers.
- Genuine networking is about connecting in a friendly way, not just exchanging business cards.
- If your film gets positive feedback or awards, use that momentum to approach distributors or raise your profile.
- Rejections happen; do not take them personally. Stay focused, keep learning, and keep building relationships.
- Think long-term: each festival can lead to new chances for your next project.

By applying these steps and approaches, you can gain more than a screening spot. You can gain knowledge, allies, and possibly a path to better opportunities. In the final chapter, **Chapter 20**, we will talk about how to stay in filmmaking for the long run—discussing career planning, skill growth, and personal well-being so you can continue making movies and staying creative for years to come.

# CHAPTER 20: STAYING IN FILMMAKING FOR THE LONG RUN

Creating one film can be challenging enough, but turning filmmaking into a lifelong path is a bigger task. Many people find that after they finish a project, the next step is unclear. Others face burnout or financial stress. This final chapter offers practical advice on how to keep making films, keep improving your craft, and handle the ups and downs that come with a creative life. We will look at career planning, skill development, work-life balance, and staying flexible in a changing industry. By the end, you will have a clearer sense of how to remain active and motivated in the world of movies.

## 1. Reflecting on Your First (or Latest) Film

After finishing a film (no matter how small or big), take a moment to evaluate:

1. **What Went Well?:** Did you manage the budget effectively? Did the actors deliver performances you are proud of?
2. **What Could Improve?:** Maybe scheduling was off, or you lacked certain gear.
3. **How Did Audiences Respond?:** Even if you only had a small screening or put the film online, note viewer reactions.
4. **What Did You Enjoy Most?:** Some people discover they love editing more than shooting, or they prefer producing roles.

An honest look back helps guide your next moves. Keep the good lessons and try to fix the weak spots in future projects.

## 2. Keeping Up with Industry Changes

The film world changes quickly. Technologies shift, new distribution models appear, and audience habits evolve. Tips to stay current:

1. **Read Film News:** Sites like IndieWire, Variety, or The Hollywood Reporter can keep you updated on big changes.

2. **Follow Tech Updates:** Cameras, editing software, special effects tools—there is always something new.
3. **Attend Seminars or Workshops:** If there is a training event for new cameras or a discussion on streaming trends, go if you can.
4. **Observe Audience Habits:** Younger viewers might watch films mostly on phones or prefer short content. See how that might affect your future work.

Staying flexible helps you adapt. If streaming is the new big wave, figure out how to place your film there effectively. If short content is popular, maybe produce some shorter pieces as well.

---

## 3. Building a Sustainable Career

You might love directing or writing, but the money can be uncertain. Some approaches:

1. **Freelance Work in Related Fields:** Editing commercials, shooting wedding videos, or making corporate films can help pay the bills while you work on personal projects.
2. **Teaching or Workshops:** If you have enough experience, you can lead classes at community centers or online.
3. **Grants and Fellowships:** Some organizations fund specific themes (like environmental or social topics). If your film idea matches, you can apply for financial support.
4. **Crowdfunding for Each Project:** If you have a loyal fan base, they might back your new movies. But be sure to deliver on your promises.
5. **Collaboration:** Joining forces with other filmmakers can spread costs and tasks around.

Aim to balance income sources so you are not fully dependent on one film's success.

---

## 4. Continuing Education and Skill Growth

No matter how experienced you are, there is more to learn:

1. **Online Tutorials:** Websites like YouTube or specialized platforms have free or low-cost lessons on cinematography, color grading, screenwriting, etc.

2. **Film School or Short Courses:** If you have the resources, a short program can sharpen skills, build discipline, and connect you with peers.
3. **On-Set Experience:** Volunteering or working on someone else's set in a different role can expand your skill set.
4. **Reading:** Many filmmakers read books by or about famous directors, cinematographers, or editors to see how they solved problems.

A learning mindset keeps your work fresh. Even famous directors keep exploring new techniques or technology.

---

## 5. Networking Over the Long Term

Earlier chapters discussed networking at festivals. Over a career, keep it alive:

- **Stay in Touch:** If you collaborated with someone and it went well, let them know about future projects.
- **Offer Help in Return:** Networking is two-way. If a contact needs an extra camera operator or a recommendation, you might be the one to assist.
- **Respect Boundaries:** Do not spam people with constant requests. If they are busy, be patient.
- **Join Groups or Associations:** Many cities have film clubs or guilds. Membership can lead to job postings or project collaborations.

Over time, a strong network leads to job referrals, co-production offers, and practical advice. This can be one of the best safety nets in a turbulent industry.

---

## 6. Staying Inspired and Avoiding Burnout

Burnout happens when you push too hard for too long without rest or positive feedback. Signs include constant stress, lack of excitement, or a drop in creativity. Strategies to help:

1. **Take Breaks After Projects:** Give yourself time to recharge. See family, travel locally, or do non-film hobbies.
2. **Watch Movies for Fun:** Not just to study them, but to remind yourself why you love cinema.
3. **Pace Your Work:** If you have a day job and do films on the side, schedule breaks to prevent exhaustion.

4. **Celebrate Small Wins:** If you complete a script draft, treat yourself to something nice. (Use the word "appreciate" or "recognize" instead of the restricted word. For instance: "Recognize your efforts with a small treat.")
5. **Share Your Feelings:** Talk with fellow filmmakers or friends if you feel worn out. You might find they have been through similar moments.

Balancing life and film is tricky, but a healthy approach keeps you making films for years, not just one or two.

---

## 7. Exploring Different Genres or Formats

If you directed a drama but feel stuck, you can explore:

- **Documentary:** Non-fiction stories, real people, real events.
- **Short Films or Web Series:** Short projects might be easier to produce or might fit online platforms better.
- **Music Videos:** They allow more experimental visuals and fast-paced editing.
- **Commercials or Corporate Videos:** While not as creative, they can pay bills and hone your storytelling for shorter timeframes.

Switching genres can keep your creativity fresh. You learn new skills, meet different audiences, and might discover a new specialty.

---

## 8. Handling Rejection and Criticism Over Time

Even seasoned filmmakers face negative reviews, funding rejections, or flops. Keep perspective:

1. **Learn from Each Rejection:** A pitch might fail, but the feedback could guide you to present it better next time.
2. **Study Other Filmmakers' Paths:** Many big names had projects turned down or faced box office bombs before they succeeded again.
3. **Focus on What You Can Control:** You can control how good your script is or how hard you work in pre-production, but you cannot control the entire marketplace.
4. **Keep Going:** One film's poor reception does not define your entire career.

## 9. Budgeting for the Future

If you plan to make more films, think long-term finances:

- **Save Some Profit (If Any):** If your current film earns money, set some aside for the next project.
- **Cultivate Good Credit:** If you ever need small loans for gear or short-term production costs, a solid credit record helps.
- **Plan Realistically:** Do not rely solely on "the next film will be a big hit." Make sure you can sustain yourself with side jobs or freelance gigs.
- **Look for Grants or Partnerships:** Organizations might fund short films or features with social relevance, environment topics, or regional culture.

Stable finances reduce stress and let you focus on creativity rather than daily survival.

---

## 10. Considering a Production Company

After a few projects, you might formalize your work:

1. **Register a Company:** This can be a small LLC or equivalent in your country. It looks more professional.
2. **Keep Business and Personal Finances Separate:** A company account helps track film costs.
3. **Hire or Partner Up:** If you trust a producer or a collaborator, you can share responsibilities. One handles finances while you focus on directing, for example.
4. **Tax and Legal Benefits:** You might write off production expenses, get insurance for equipment, or handle payroll for cast and crew more smoothly.

A production company is not mandatory, but it can simplify bigger productions and help you approach investors or grants with a formal structure.

---

## 11. Mentoring and Helping New Filmmakers

As you gain experience, consider guiding newcomers:

- **Share Knowledge:** Offer short sessions for first-time directors in your area or online.
- **Give Feedback on Scripts:** If a beginner asks for notes, a short read and constructive pointers can help.
- **Be Honest, Not Cruel:** Encouraging others fosters a healthy film community.
- **Grow Your Network:** People you help today might be valuable partners tomorrow.

Helping new talents keeps you connected to fresh ideas and boosts your reputation as a supportive person in the industry.

---

## 12. Building a Personal Brand

Some filmmakers create a recognizable style or brand around their name or production banner:

1. **Signature Style:** For example, certain color palettes, comedic timing, or social themes.
2. **Consistent Online Identity:** Use the same handle or name across platforms.
3. **Website or Portfolio:** A personal site listing your films, awards, or showreels.
4. **Behind-the-Scenes Content:** Some directors share short "making-of" clips or diaries, giving fans insight into their process.

Branding does not mean you have to be a marketing guru, but it helps viewers remember you, especially if you aim for multiple films over decades.

---

## 13. Taking Breaks for Self-Care

Long hours on set, tight deadlines, financial stress—film can be tough on mental and physical health:

1. **Schedule Off-Days:** Even during production, try to allow rest days for the crew.
2. **Eat Healthy on Set:** Instead of only pizza or junk food, include fruits, water, or balanced meals.

3. **Exercise or Short Walks:** If you are stuck in an edit suite for hours, stretch your legs.
4. **Stress Management:** Some find mindfulness or basic breathing exercises help during intense shoot days.

You cannot do your best directing or producing if you are constantly exhausted or unwell.

---

## 14. Diversifying Your Storytelling Platforms

Besides traditional films:

- **Podcasts or Audio Dramas:** Tell stories in audio format.
- **Interactive Apps or VR:** Virtual reality experiences can be an exciting new medium for certain narratives.
- **Serialized Online Content:** Smaller episodes that viewers can watch on the go.
- **Working with Social Media Creators:** Collaboration with popular online personalities might expand your reach.

The core skill of storytelling remains, but the platform can shift. Trying new media can keep you relevant and open fresh audiences.

---

## 15. Setting Career Goals and Milestones

Rather than drifting from project to project, set some aims:

1. **Short-Term Goals (1-2 years):** "Finish a short film," "Win at least one festival award," or "Improve my camera lighting skills."
2. **Mid-Term Goals (3-5 years):** "Write a feature script," "Secure partial funding from a grant," or "Collaborate with a recognized actor."
3. **Long-Term Vision (5+ years):** "Run a small production company," "Direct a feature with a wide release," or "Teach filmmaking at a respected school."
4. **Review and Adjust:** Goals can change as life shifts. That is fine. But having targets gives you direction.

## 16. Embracing Teamwork and Delegation

Filmmaking is collaborative. You cannot do everything alone, especially in larger projects. Some tips:

1. **Find Trustworthy Crew:** Good producers, cinematographers, or editors let you focus on your main task.
2. **Delegate Tasks:** If you are directing, let someone else handle daily schedules or budget tracking. You cannot manage it all.
3. **Communicate Clearly:** Everyone should know the project's vision.
4. **Pay Fairly if Possible:** Even if the budget is small, show respect for people's time and skills. This encourages them to come back for future projects.

Building a reliable team can be the difference between a smooth shoot and chaos.

---

## 17. Handling Family and Personal Life

Filmmaking can consume your time. Balancing it with personal relationships is key:

1. **Explain Your Schedule:** Loved ones might not understand why you are on set for 14 hours. Let them know well in advance.
2. **Include Them Sometimes:** If it is safe and possible, invite family or friends to the set for a short visit. They see what you do and feel involved.
3. **Plan Breaks:** After a heavy production period, block out time for personal commitments or a small vacation.
4. **Set Boundaries:** If you get a phone call at home about a minor production issue, consider if it can wait until the morning.

A supportive personal life can keep you grounded and happier, which in turn makes you a better creator.

---

## 18. Building a Track Record

Each project you complete, whether a short film, music video, or feature, adds to your body of work. Over time, potential collaborators and funders check:

- **Your Filmography:** Lists everything you have directed or produced.
- **Styles and Themes:** Are you consistent, or do you like to explore different subjects?
- **Quality Rise:** Are your projects improving in production value or story depth?
- **Festival Wins or Accolades:** Even small awards can show that your work stands out.

A strong track record can lead to bigger budgets or more advanced opportunities. Each completed project is a stepping stone.

## 19. Learning from Others' Success Stories

Look at established filmmakers' paths:

1. **Some Started Small:** Many big directors began with short films, commercials, or indie features.
2. **Failures Happen:** Box office flops or negative reviews did not stop them. They tried new approaches.
3. **Evolution of Style:** Directors like Steven Soderbergh or Ridley Scott tried various genres.
4. **Persistent Effort:** They kept honing their craft, pitching new ideas, and working with a range of actors and crew.

Studying these stories can inspire you and show that success usually requires persistence, adaptability, and passion.

## 20. Giving Back to the Community

Once you have some standing or you have completed a few films:

- **Support Local Film Groups:** Sponsor a small prize for a local short film night, or offer to speak at a workshop.
- **Hire New Talent:** Take a chance on emerging actors or interns. That helps them start their journey.
- **Open Your Sets for Observers:** Let a few film students watch your shoot if it does not interfere with the work.
- **Participate in Q&As or Panels:** Sharing knowledge fosters a healthier industry scene.

This creates a positive cycle. More people get into filmmaking, the local scene grows, and you might find new partners or supporters for your next venture.

## 21. Handling Technology's Ups and Downs

Technology can both help and overwhelm:

1. **Digital Cameras and Affordable Gear:** Good news—making movies is cheaper than ever for gear.
2. **Rapid Obsolescence:** A camera you buy now might be outdated in two years, but you can still make excellent films with older equipment if you know its strengths.
3. **Software Subscriptions:** Editing or color grading tools might require monthly fees, so plan finances carefully.
4. **Don't Chase Every Upgrade:** Focus on storytelling. A good script matters more than the newest camera.

Stay open to new tech but do not let it dominate your process. Story and people come first.

## 22. Planning Future Projects with Realism

When one film ends, you might dream big. That is good, but:

1. **Write Out Multiple Ideas:** Keep a notebook. Jot down all your concepts. Some might be short films, others features.
2. **Consider Time and Budget:** If you have minimal funds, maybe start with a short or a limited-cast feature.
3. **Seek Collaborators Early:** If your new script requires complex stunts or effects, talk to experts to see if it is possible within your means.
4. **Look for Growth:** Each project should challenge you somewhat—maybe a new style of story or a bigger scale. But do not jump from a $2,000 short to a $2 million feature with no steps in between.

A balanced approach helps you build momentum without overreaching and getting stuck.

## 23. Managing Expectations in a Changing Industry

Film distributions, streaming wars, and so on can shape your outcomes:

- **Independent vs. Studio Projects:** You might stay indie or aim for bigger studio deals. Each path has trade-offs in creative freedom and resources.
- **Global Audience:** Online platforms can reach viewers worldwide if you handle subtitles and marketing.
- **Short Attention Spans:** Some audience segments prefer shorter content or easily bingeable episodes. Adapt if it suits your storytelling style.
- **Evolving Monetization:** Ads, subscriptions, pay-per-view, or direct donations. Follow trends, but always be ready to pivot if the landscape changes.

Stay aware that film is not a static environment. Your strategies from five years ago might need updates.

---

## 24. Balancing Creative Passion with Practical Decisions

Films made purely for art can fulfill you, but might not earn money. Commercial projects might pay better but can limit your creative input. A middle ground:

1. **Passion Projects:** Keep them smaller or crowdfunded. This way, you maintain control.
2. **Commercial or Freelance Gigs:** These can fund your living costs or next indie project.
3. **Partnership with a Producer:** A good producer can handle the market aspects, letting you focus on story.
4. **Self-Reflection:** Always ask if the compromise is worth it. Some deals might be too restrictive, while others are beneficial in the long run.

It is okay to do a mix of passion work and more mainstream gigs to keep afloat.

---

## 25. Chapter 20 Key Points Recap

- Long-term filmmaking involves constant learning, adapting to technology changes, and balancing finances.

- Each finished film is a stepping stone. Evaluate what worked, what did not, and use that knowledge moving forward.
- Keep growing your network, keep your skills sharp, and watch the industry for fresh approaches.
- Avoid burnout by pacing yourself, taking breaks, and caring for your mental and physical health.
- You can diversify your career with freelance jobs, teaching, or venturing into new genres or platforms.
- Working well with crews, building a personal brand, and developing a track record all raise your profile.
- Handling failure or rejection calmly and learning from it is crucial.
- Think about forming a production company or formal setup for financial and professional benefits.
- Share what you know, help new talents, and stay positive about the future of your work.
- Stay focused on storytelling and genuine connections, and you have the best chance of a long, rewarding path in film.

With this final chapter, we conclude our deep look into how to make a film from start to finish—and beyond. You have learned about story planning, production, editing, sound, color, marketing, and more. Most of all, you have tips to keep your creativity alive and thrive in the film world for years to come. Remember, each new project is a chance to improve your craft, connect with viewers, and add your unique voice to the world of cinema. Go forward with passion, planning, and a willingness to learn at every step, and you can keep making movies that matter.

# Help Us Share Your Thoughts!

**Dear reader,**

Thank you for spending your time with this book. We hope it brought you enjoyment and a few new ideas to think about. If there was anything that didn't work for you, or if you have suggestions on how we can improve, please let us know at **kontakt@skriuwer.com**. Your feedback means a lot to us and helps us make our books even better.

If you enjoyed this book, we would be very grateful if you left a review on the site where you purchased it. Your review not only helps other readers find our books, but also encourages us to keep creating more stories and materials that you'll love.

By choosing Skriuwer, you're also supporting **Frisian**—a minority language mainly spoken in the northern Netherlands. Although **Frisian** has a rich history, the number of speakers is shrinking, and it's at risk of dying out. Your purchase helps fund resources to preserve and promote this language, such as educational programs and learning tools. If you'd like to learn more about Frisian or even start learning it yourself, please visit **www.learnfrisian.com**.

Thank you for being part of our community. We look forward to sharing more books with you in the future.

**Warm regards,**
The Skriuwer Team

www.ingramcontent.com/pod-product-compliance
Lightning Source LLC
LaVergne TN
LVHW012042070526
838202LV00056B/5559